THE SCHOOL MATHEMATICS P[...]

ADVANCED TABLE[...]

SECOND EDITION

CW00751146

CONTENTS

CAMBRIDGE UNIVERSITY PRESS

Published by the Syndics of the Cambridge University Press
Bentley House, 200 Euston Road, London NW1 2DB
American Branch: 32 East 57th Street, New York, N.Y.10022

© Cambridge University Press 1966

This edition © Cambridge University Press 1971

ISBN: 0 521 08203 X

This edition first published 1971
Reprinted 1973 1974 1975

PUBLISHER'S NOTE

The second edition of these tables has been printed in an enlarged page size. The formula section and some of the tables have been considerably expanded. Tables of $\sinh^{-1}x$ and $\cosh^{-1}x$ are now included but a few little-used tables from the first edition have been omitted.

Printed in Great Britain
at the University Printing House, Cambridge
(Euan Phillips, University Printer)

ARRANGEMENT OF DEFINITIONS AND FORMULAE

DEFINITIONS AND FORMULAE

Area and volume formulae

Volume of a cone or pyramid $= \frac{1}{3}Ah$, where $A =$ base area, $h =$ height of vertex.
Area of curved surface of a cone $= \pi rl$, where $l =$ slant height.
Volume of a sphere $= \frac{4}{3}\pi r^3$.
Surface area of a sphere $= 4\pi r^2$.
Area of a spherical zone
(between planes distance h apart) $= 2\pi rh$.

Trigonometry

$$\sec\theta = \frac{1}{\cos\theta}; \quad \csc\theta = \frac{1}{\sin\theta}; \quad \cot\theta = \frac{1}{\tan\theta}.$$

$$\cos^2\theta + \sin^2\theta = 1; \quad 1 + \tan^2\theta = \sec^2\theta; \quad \cot^2\theta + 1 = \csc^2\theta.$$

$$\sin(\theta \pm \phi) = \sin\theta\cos\phi \pm \cos\theta\sin\phi; \quad \cos(\theta \pm \phi) = \cos\theta\cos\phi \mp \sin\theta\sin\phi;$$

$$\tan(\theta \pm \phi) = \frac{\tan\theta \pm \tan\phi}{1 \mp \tan\theta\tan\phi} \quad [\theta \pm \phi \neq (k + \tfrac{1}{2})\pi].$$

$$\sin 2\theta = 2\sin\theta\cos\theta; \quad \cos 2\theta = \cos^2\theta - \sin^2\theta; \quad \tan 2\theta = \frac{2\tan\theta}{1 - \tan^2\theta} \quad [\theta \neq (\tfrac{1}{2}k + \tfrac{1}{4})\pi].$$

$$2\cos^2\theta = 1 + \cos 2\theta; \quad 2\sin^2\theta = 1 - \cos 2\theta.$$

If $t = \tan\frac{1}{2}\theta$, then $\sin\theta = \dfrac{2t}{1+t^2}; \quad \cos\theta = \dfrac{1-t^2}{1+t^2}; \quad \tan\theta = \dfrac{2t}{1-t^2}; \quad \dfrac{d\theta}{dt} = \dfrac{2}{1+t^2}.$

$$2\sin\theta\cos\phi = \sin(\theta+\phi) + \sin(\theta-\phi);$$

$$2\cos\theta\cos\phi = \cos(\theta+\phi) + \cos(\theta-\phi);$$

$$2\sin\theta\sin\phi = \cos(\theta-\phi) - \cos(\theta+\phi).$$

$$\sin\alpha + \sin\beta = 2\sin\tfrac{1}{2}(\alpha+\beta)\cos\tfrac{1}{2}(\alpha-\beta); \quad \sin\alpha - \sin\beta = 2\cos\tfrac{1}{2}(\alpha+\beta)\sin\tfrac{1}{2}(\alpha-\beta);$$

$$\cos\alpha + \cos\beta = 2\cos\tfrac{1}{2}(\alpha+\beta)\cos\tfrac{1}{2}(\alpha-\beta); \quad \cos\alpha - \cos\beta = 2\sin\tfrac{1}{2}(\alpha+\beta)\sin\tfrac{1}{2}(\beta-\alpha).$$

In the triangle ABC:

$$\frac{a}{\sin A} = \frac{b}{\sin B} = \frac{c}{\sin C} = 2R;$$

$$a^2 = b^2 + c^2 - 2bc\cos A, \text{ etc.};$$

$$\tan\tfrac{1}{2}A = \sqrt{\frac{(s-b)(s-c)}{s(s-a)}}, \text{ etc.}; \quad \triangle = \sqrt{\{s(s-a)(s-b)(s-c)\}};$$

where $s = \frac{1}{2}(a+b+c)$.

Ranges of the inverse functions:

$$-\tfrac{1}{2}\pi \leqslant \sin^{-1}x \leqslant \tfrac{1}{2}\pi; \quad 0 \leqslant \cos^{-1}x \leqslant \pi; \quad -\tfrac{1}{2}\pi < \tan^{-1}x < \tfrac{1}{2}\pi.$$

DEFINITIONS AND FORMULAE

Algebra

Series

$$\sum_{i=1}^{n} i = \tfrac{1}{2}n(n+1) \quad \text{(an } \textit{arithmetic progression} \text{)}.$$

$$\sum_{i=1}^{n} i^2 = \tfrac{1}{6}n(n+1)(2n+1); \quad \sum_{i=1}^{n} i^3 = \tfrac{1}{4}n^2(n+1)^2.$$

$$\sum_{i=1}^{n} i(i+1)(i+2)\ldots(i+r) = \frac{1}{r+2}\,n(n+1)(n+2)\ldots(n+r+1).$$

$$\sum_{i=1}^{n} x^{i-1} = \frac{1-x^n}{1-x} \quad (x \neq 1) \quad \text{(a } \textit{geometric progression} \text{)}; \text{ if } |x| < 1,\ \sum_{i=1}^{\infty} x^{i-1} = \frac{1}{1-x}.$$

Binomial coefficients

If i is a natural number,

$$\binom{n}{i} = \frac{n(n-1)\ldots(n-i+1)}{i!}.$$

Coefficients may be calculated from the definition

$$\binom{n}{0} = 1, \quad \binom{n}{i+1} = \frac{n-i}{i+1}\binom{n}{i}$$

Also,

$$\binom{k+1}{i} = \binom{k}{i-1} + \binom{k}{i}.$$

If n is also a natural number, and if $_nC_i$ denotes the number of subsets of i elements contained in a set of n elements, then

$$_nC_i = \binom{n}{i} = \frac{n!}{i!(n-i)!}.$$

The *binomial theorem*: If n is a natural number,

$$(b+a)^n = \sum_{i=0}^{n} \binom{n}{i} b^{n-i}a^i.$$

Logarithms, exponentials and hyperbolic functions

$y = b^x \Leftrightarrow x = \log_b y.$

$y = \exp x \Leftrightarrow x = \ln y$ ($\exp x$ is the same as e^x, $\ln y$ as $\log_e y$).

$q^x = \exp(x \ln q).$

$\log_b a = \log_c a/\log_c b$; in particular, $\ln a = \log_{10} a/\log_{10} e \approx 2{\cdot}3026 \log_{10} a.$

$\sinh x = \tfrac{1}{2}(e^x - e^{-x}); \quad \cosh x = \tfrac{1}{2}(e^x + e^{-x}); \quad \tanh x = \sinh x/\cosh x.$

$\sinh^{-1} x = \ln\{x + \sqrt{(1+x^2)}\}; \quad \cosh^{-1} x = \ln\{x + \sqrt{(x^2-1)}\} \quad (x \geqslant 1);$

$\tanh^{-1} x = \tfrac{1}{2}\ln\{(1+x)/(1-x)\} \quad (-1 < x < 1).$

Quadratic functions

If $a \neq 0$,

$$ax^2 + bx + c = 0 \iff x = \frac{-b \pm \sqrt{(b^2 - 4ac)}}{2a}.$$

Sum of roots $= -b/a$; product of roots $= c/a$.

In real algebra, if $a \neq 0$,

$$ax^2 + bx + c > 0 \quad \text{for all } x \iff a > 0 \text{ and } 4ac - b^2 > 0.$$

[3]

DEFINITIONS AND FORMULAE

Complex numbers

If $z = a+bj$ (a, b real), then the modulus $|z|$ and the argument $\arg z$ are defined by:

$$|z| = \sqrt{(a^2+b^2)}; \arg z \text{ is the number such that } -\pi < \arg z \leqslant \pi \text{ whose sine is } b/|z|$$
$$\text{and whose cosine is } a/|z| \ (z \neq 0).$$

The conjugate complex number z^* (also often written $\bar{z}$) is $z^* = a-bj$, so that $zz^* = |z|^2$, $z+z^* = 2\,\mathrm{re}\,z$.

If $z = r(\cos\theta + j\sin\theta)$ (r, θ real, $r > 0$), then $|z| = r$, $\arg z = \theta + 2k\pi$, where k is an integer chosen so that $-\pi < \arg z \leqslant \pi$. This form can also be written $z = re^{\theta j}$, or $r\exp(\theta j)$.

De Moivre's theorem for integral index:

$$(\cos\theta + j\sin\theta)^n = \cos n\theta + j\sin n\theta.$$

The roots of $x^n = 1$ are $x = \exp\{2\pi(k/n)j\}$ for $k = 0, 1, 2, ..., n-1$. In particular, the roots of $x^3 = 1$ are $1, \omega, \omega^2$, where

$$\omega = \cos\tfrac{2}{3}\pi + j\sin\tfrac{2}{3}\pi = -\tfrac{1}{2} + (\tfrac{1}{2}\sqrt{3})j,$$

so that $\omega^3 = 1$ and $1+\omega+\omega^2 = 0$.

Binary operations on a set

Denoting the set by S and the operation by $\circ$:

The set is *closed* with respect to the operation if, for all a, $b \in S$, $a \circ b \in S$.

A *neutral element* (or *identity*) is an element $e \in S$ such that, for all $a \in S$, $e \circ a = a \circ e = a$.

The *inverse* of an element $a \in S$ is an element $a' \in S$ such that $a \circ a' = a' \circ a = e$.

The operation is *associative* if, for all a, b, $c \in S$, $a \circ (b \circ c) = (a \circ b) \circ c$.

The operation is *commutative* if, for all a, $b \in S$, $a \circ b = b \circ a$.

For two operations $\circ$, $*$:

The operation $\circ$ is *distributive* over the operation $*$ if, for all a, b, $c \in S$,

$$a \circ (b * c) = (a \circ b) * (a \circ c) \quad \text{and} \quad (b * c) \circ a = (b \circ a) * (c \circ a).$$

Relations between elements of a set

Denoting the set by S and the relation by R:

The relation is *reflexive* if, for all $a \in S$, aRa.

The relation is *symmetric* if, for all a, $b \in S$, $aRb \Rightarrow bRa$.

The relation is *transitive* if, for all a, b, $c \in S$, (aRb and bRc) $\Rightarrow aRc$.

An *equivalence relation* is a relation which is reflexive, symmetric and transitive.

Algebraic structures

1. GROUP $(S, \circ)$

> *Single binary operation* $\circ$
> S closed under $\circ$
> $\circ$ is associative
> Neutral element exists
> Every element has an inverse

2. ABELIAN GROUP $(S, \circ)$

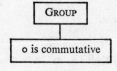

DEFINITIONS AND FORMULAE

3. RING $(S, +, .)$

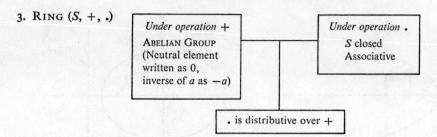

Under operation $+$	Under operation $.$
ABELIAN GROUP (Neutral element written as 0, inverse of a as $-a$)	S closed Associative

$.$ is distributive over $+$

4. INTEGRAL DOMAIN $(S, +, .)$

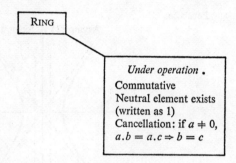

RING

Under operation $.$
Commutative
Neutral element exists
(written as 1)
Cancellation: if $a \neq 0$,
$a.b = a.c \Rightarrow b = c$

5. FIELD $(S, +, .)$

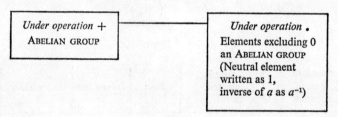

Under operation $+$	Under operation $.$
ABELIAN GROUP	Elements excluding 0 an ABELIAN GROUP (Neutral element written as 1, inverse of a as a^{-1})

6. VECTOR SPACE $S = \{a, b, c \ldots\}$ over a field $F = (\{\lambda, \mu, \nu \ldots\}, +, .)$

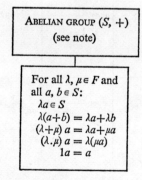

ABELIAN GROUP $(S, +)$
(see note)

For all $\lambda, \mu \in F$ and
all $a, b \in S$:
$\lambda a \in S$
$\lambda(a+b) = \lambda a + \lambda b$
$(\lambda + \mu) a = \lambda a + \mu a$
$(\lambda . \mu) a = \lambda(\mu a)$
$1a = a$

Note. Strictly, this binary operation $+$ is not the same $+$ as in the field F, since it operates on a different set of elements. It is, however, customary to use the same symbol for the two. The elements of S are called vectors, and the elements of F scalars.

Relations between structures

An *isomorphism* between two groups $(G, *)$ and $(H, \circ)$ is a one–one mapping such that, if $a \leftrightarrow x$ and $b \leftrightarrow y$ (where $a, b \in G$, $x, y \in H$), then $a * b \leftrightarrow x \circ y$.

A *homomorphism* between two groups $(G, *)$ and $(H, \circ)$ is a mapping such that, if $a \to x$ and $b \to y$, then $a * b \to x \circ y$.

Isomorphisms and homomorphisms between other pairs of structures are defined similarly.

[5]

DEFINITIONS AND FORMULAE

Conics

Classification

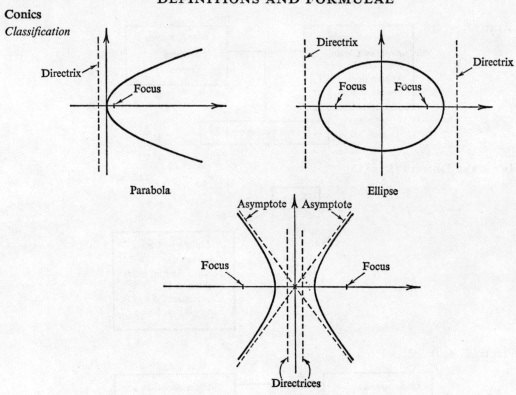

Parabola

Ellipse

Hyperbola

Name of curve	Standard form of equation	Standard parametric forms	Foci	Directrices	Eccentricity	Asymptotes
Parabola	$y^2 = 4ax$	$(ap^2, 2ap)$	$(a, 0)$	$x = -a$	$e = 1$	None
Ellipse	$\dfrac{x^2}{a^2} + \dfrac{y^2}{b^2} = 1$	$(a\cos\theta,\ b\sin\theta)$ or $\left(a\dfrac{1-p^2}{1+p^2},\ b\dfrac{2p}{1+p^2}\right)$ where $p = \tan\frac{1}{2}\theta$	$(\pm ae, 0)$	$x = \pm\dfrac{a}{e}$	$e = \dfrac{\sqrt{(a^2-b^2)}}{a}$ < 1	None
Hyperbola	$\dfrac{x^2}{a^2} - \dfrac{y^2}{b^2} = 1$	$(a\sec\phi,\ b\tan\phi)$ or $\dfrac{a}{2}\left(p+\dfrac{1}{p}\right),\ \dfrac{b}{2}\left(p-\dfrac{1}{p}\right)$ where $p = \tan\frac{1}{2}(\frac{1}{2}\pi-\phi)$	$(\pm ae, 0)$	$x = \pm\dfrac{a}{e}$	$e = \dfrac{\sqrt{(a^2+b^2)}}{a}$ > 1	$\dfrac{x}{a} \pm \dfrac{y}{b} = 0$

General second degree equation

$$ax^2 + 2hxy + by^2 + 2gx + 2fy + c = 0$$

is the equation of a parabola, ellipse or hyperbola according as $ab - h^2 = 0$, > 0 or < 0.

The equation represents a degenerate conic if and only if

$$\begin{vmatrix} a & h & g \\ h & b & f \\ g & f & c \end{vmatrix} = 0.$$

[6]

DEFINITIONS AND FORMULAE

Polar equation

If the origin is taken at a focus of the conic, and the line $\theta = 0$ as the ray from that focus drawn towards the corresponding directrix, then the equation of the conic has the form

$$\frac{l}{r} = 1 + e \cos \theta,$$

where e is the eccentricity and l the length of the semi-latus rectum.

Vectors

Products

If $\mathbf{a}$, $\mathbf{b}$ are two vectors in three-dimensional space with magnitudes a, b, and if the angle between them is θ (where $0 \leqslant \theta \leqslant \pi$), then:

$\mathbf{a.b}$ is a scalar of magnitude $ab \cos \theta$;

$\mathbf{a} \times \mathbf{b}$ is a vector of magnitude $ab \sin \theta$, in a direction perpendicular to both $\mathbf{a}$ and $\mathbf{b}$ such that $\mathbf{a}, \mathbf{b}, \mathbf{a} \times \mathbf{b}$ form a right-handed triple.

If the vectors $\mathbf{a}$, $\mathbf{b}$ are represented by column matrices $\begin{pmatrix} a_1 \\ a_2 \\ a_3 \end{pmatrix}$, $\begin{pmatrix} b_1 \\ b_2 \\ b_3 \end{pmatrix}$ of their components with respect to a rectangular system of right-handed axes, then:

$$\mathbf{a.b} = a_1 b_1 + a_2 b_2 + a_3 b_3;$$

$$\mathbf{a} \times \mathbf{b} = \begin{pmatrix} a_2 b_3 - a_3 b_2 \\ a_3 b_1 - a_1 b_3 \\ a_1 b_2 - a_2 b_1 \end{pmatrix} = \begin{vmatrix} \hat{\imath} & \hat{\jmath} & \hat{\mathbf{k}} \\ a_1 & a_2 & a_3 \\ b_1 & b_2 & b_3 \end{vmatrix}.$$

Scalar triple product:

$$\mathbf{a.(b \times c)} = \mathbf{b.(c \times a)} = \mathbf{c.(a \times b)} = \begin{vmatrix} a_1 & b_1 & c_1 \\ a_2 & b_2 & c_2 \\ a_3 & b_3 & c_3 \end{vmatrix} \quad \text{(written } [\mathbf{abc}]).$$

Vector triple product:

$$\mathbf{a \times (b \times c)} = \mathbf{(a.c)b - (a.b)c}; \quad \mathbf{(a \times b) \times c} = \mathbf{(a.c)b - (b.c)a}.$$

DEFINITIONS AND FORMULAE

Planes and lines

[**a, b, c, p** stand for the position vectors of points A, B, C, P relative to an origin. The results apply only in non-degenerate situations: two points A, B are not coincident, three points A, B, C are not collinear.]

P lies on the line $AB \Leftrightarrow \mathbf{p} = \lambda\mathbf{a} + \mu\mathbf{b}$ with $\lambda + \mu = 1$. (P is then the point of the line with the property that

$$AP/PB = \mu/\lambda, \quad \lambda \neq 0.)$$

P lies on the plane $ABC \Leftrightarrow \mathbf{p} = \lambda\mathbf{a} + \mu\mathbf{b} + \nu\mathbf{c}$ with $\lambda + \mu + \nu = 1$.

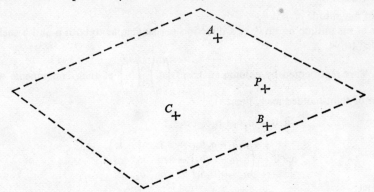

P lies on the line through A with direction given by the vector $\mathbf{l} \Leftrightarrow \mathbf{p} = \mathbf{a} + t\mathbf{l}$.

In Cartesian form,
$$\begin{pmatrix} x \\ y \\ z \end{pmatrix} = \begin{pmatrix} a_1 \\ a_2 \\ a_3 \end{pmatrix} + t \begin{pmatrix} l_1 \\ l_2 \\ l_3 \end{pmatrix}.$$

P lies on the plane through A with normal given by the vector $\mathbf{n} \Leftrightarrow \mathbf{n}.(\mathbf{p} - \mathbf{a}) = 0$.

In Cartesian form,
$$n_1 x + n_2 y + n_3 z = n_1 a_1 + n_2 a_2 + n_3 a_3.$$

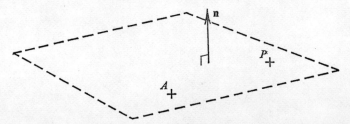

The distance from the point P_1 to the plane with equation $\mathbf{n}.\mathbf{p} = k$ is $|\mathbf{n}.\mathbf{p}_1 - k|/n$, where n is the magnitude of the normal vector $\mathbf{n}$.

In *two dimensions*, the equation $\mathbf{n}.(\mathbf{p} - \mathbf{a}) = 0$ gives the set of points P on the line through A with normal given by the vector $\mathbf{n}$; and $|\mathbf{n}.\mathbf{p}_1 - k|/n$ is the distance from the point P_1 to the line with equation $\mathbf{n}.\mathbf{p} = k$.

Referred to rectangular axes, the equation of the line through A making an angle α with the x axis is
$$\begin{pmatrix} x \\ y \end{pmatrix} = \begin{pmatrix} a_1 \\ a_2 \end{pmatrix} + t \begin{pmatrix} \cos\alpha \\ \sin\alpha \end{pmatrix},$$

or
$$y - a_2 = \tan\alpha(x - a_1);$$

and the equation of the line through A whose normal makes an angle β with the x axis is
$$x\cos\beta + y\sin\beta = a_1\cos\beta + a_2\sin\beta.$$

Differentiation

If $\dfrac{f(x)-f(a)}{x-a}$ tends to a limit as x tends to a, then f is said to be differentiable at a. The limit is called the derivative of f at a and is usually written $f'(a)$. The function f' is called the derived function of f.

Derivatives of common functions

$f(x)$	$f'(x)$
x^m	mx^{m-1}
$\sin x$	$\cos x$
$\cos x$	$-\sin x$
$\tan x$	$\sec^2 x$
$\sec x$	$\sec x \tan x$
$\cot x$	$-\csc^2 x$
$\csc x$	$-\csc x \cot x$
$e^x \,(= \exp x)$	$e^x \,(= \exp x)$
a^x	$\ln a . a^x$
$\ln x \,(= \log_e x)$	$1/x$
$\sinh x$	$\cosh x$
$\cosh x$	$\sinh x$

If $y = uv$, then
$$\frac{dy}{dx} = \frac{du}{dx}v + u\frac{dv}{dx}.$$

If $y = u/v$, then
$$\frac{dy}{dx} = \left(\frac{du}{dx}v - u\frac{dv}{dx}\right)\Big/ v^2.$$

Approximations to derivatives

If the derivatives exist, then for small h

$$f'(x) \approx \frac{f(x+h)-f(x-h)}{2h};$$

$$f''(x) \approx \frac{f(x+h)-2f(x)+f(x-h)}{h^2}.$$

Polynomial approximations to functions

Taylor's approximation. For small α,

$$f(p+\alpha) \approx f(p)+f'(p).\alpha+\frac{1}{2!}f''(p).\alpha^2+\ldots+\frac{1}{m!}f^{(m)}(p).\alpha^m,$$

provided that the derivatives exist and are continuous at p.

Applications to particular functions:

$$(1+\alpha)^n \approx 1+n\alpha+\frac{n(n-1)}{2!}\alpha^2+\ldots+\binom{n}{m}\alpha^m.$$

$$\ln(1+\alpha) \approx \alpha-\frac{\alpha^2}{2}+\frac{\alpha^3}{3}-\ldots+(-1)^{m+1}\frac{\alpha^m}{m}.$$

$$e^\alpha \approx 1+\alpha+\frac{\alpha^2}{2!}+\ldots+\frac{\alpha^m}{m!}.$$

$$\cosh\alpha \approx 1+\frac{\alpha^2}{2!}+\frac{\alpha^4}{4!}+\ldots+\frac{\alpha^{2k}}{(2k)!}.$$

$$\sinh\alpha \approx \alpha+\frac{\alpha^3}{3!}+\ldots+\frac{\alpha^{2k+1}}{(2k+1)!}.$$

$$\cos\alpha \approx 1-\frac{\alpha^2}{2!}+\frac{\alpha^4}{4!}+\ldots+(-1)^k\frac{\alpha^{2k}}{(2k)!}.$$

$$\sin\alpha \approx \alpha-\frac{\alpha^3}{3!}+\ldots+(-1)^k\frac{\alpha^{2k+1}}{(2k+1)!}.$$

DEFINITIONS AND FORMULAE

Power series with intervals of validity

$$(1+x)^n = \sum_{i=0}^{\infty} \binom{n}{i} x^i \quad \text{for} \quad |x| < 1,$$

and sometimes also for $x = 1$ and/or $x = -1$. [Note that, if n is a positive integer, then the series terminates and the equation holds for all x; this is the *binomial theorem* (see p. 3).]

$$\ln(1+x) = \sum_{i=1}^{\infty} (-1)^{i+1} \frac{x^i}{i} \quad \text{for} \quad -1 < x \leqslant 1.$$

$$e^x = \sum_{i=0}^{\infty} \frac{x^i}{i!} \quad \text{for all } x.$$

$$\cosh x = \sum_{i=0}^{\infty} \frac{x^{2i}}{(2i)!}, \quad \sinh x = \sum_{i=0}^{\infty} \frac{x^{2i+1}}{(2i+1)!} \quad \text{for all } x.$$

$$\cos x = \sum_{i=0}^{\infty} (-1)^i \frac{x^{2i}}{(2i)!}, \quad \sin x = \sum_{i=0}^{\infty} (-1)^i \frac{x^{2i+1}}{(2i+1)!} \quad \text{for all } x.$$

Newton–Raphson method

If p is an approximation to a root of $f(x) = 0$, then $p - \dfrac{f(p)}{f'(p)}$ is generally a better approximation.

Differential geometry

[Primes denote differentiation with respect to a parameter.]

Arc length: $\qquad (s')^2 = (x')^2 + (y')^2; \quad (s')^2 = (r')^2 + (r\theta')^2.$

Tangential direction: $\qquad \cos \psi = dx/ds, \quad \sin \psi = dy/ds;$

$$\cos \phi = dr/ds, \quad \sin \phi = r\, d\theta/ds.$$

Curvature: $\qquad \kappa = \dfrac{d\psi}{ds} = \dfrac{x'y'' - x''y'}{\{(x')^2 + (y')^2\}^{\frac{3}{2}}}.$

Radius of curvature $\rho = 1/\kappa.$

Integration

Approximations to definite integrals

[In these formulae $x_n = x_0 + nh$ and $y_i = f(x_i)$.]

Trapezium rule: $\qquad \displaystyle\int_{x_0}^{x_n} f(x)\,dx \approx \tfrac{1}{2}h\{(y_0 + y_n) + 2(y_1 + y_2 + \ldots + y_{n-1})\}.$

Simpson's rule, in which n must be *even*, giving an *odd* number of ordinates:

$$\int_{x_0}^{x_n} f(x)\,dx \approx \tfrac{1}{3}h\{(y_0 + y_n) + 4(y_1 + y_3 + \ldots + y_{n-1}) + 2(y_2 + y_4 + \ldots + y_{n-2})\}.$$

DEFINITIONS AND FORMULAE

Primitives (indefinite integrals) of common functions

[In the following we take $a > 0$ and omit the additive constant.]

$f(x)$	$\int f(x)\,dx$
$x^n\ (n \neq -1)$	$x^{n+1}/(n+1)$
$1/x$	$\ln x$ if $x > 0$, $\ln(-x)$ if $x < 0$ (i.e. $\ln|x|$, $x \neq 0$)
$\dfrac{1}{x^2+a^2}$	$\dfrac{1}{a}\tan^{-1}\dfrac{x}{a}$
$\dfrac{1}{x^2-a^2}$	$\dfrac{1}{2a}\ln\left|\dfrac{x-a}{x+a}\right|$
$\dfrac{1}{\sqrt{(x^2+a^2)}}$	$\sinh^{-1}\dfrac{x}{a}$
$\dfrac{1}{\sqrt{(x^2-a^2)}}$	$\cosh^{-1}\dfrac{x}{a}$
$\dfrac{1}{\sqrt{(a^2-x^2)}}$	$\sin^{-1}\dfrac{x}{a}$
$\sin x$	$-\cos x$
$\cos x$	$\sin x$
$\tan x$	$\ln|\sec x|$
$\cot x$	$\ln|\sin x|$
$\sec x$	$\ln|\sec x+\tan x| = \ln|\tan(\tfrac{1}{2}x+\tfrac{1}{4}\pi)|$
$\csc x$	$\ln|\tan\tfrac{1}{2}x|$
$e^{ax}\sin bx$	$\dfrac{e^{ax}}{a^2+b^2}(a\sin bx - b\cos bx)$
$e^{ax}\cos bx$	$\dfrac{e^{ax}}{a^2+b^2}(a\cos bx + b\sin bx)$
$\sin^2 x$	$\tfrac{1}{2}(x - \tfrac{1}{2}\sin 2x)$
$\cos^2 x$	$\tfrac{1}{2}(x + \tfrac{1}{2}\sin 2x)$
$\sinh x$	$\cosh x$
$\cosh x$	$\sinh x$

For the $\sinh^{-1}\dfrac{x}{a}$ and $\cosh^{-1}\dfrac{x}{a}$ entries: For logarithmic forms of inverse hyperbolic functions, see p. 3.

Integration by parts

$$\int u\,\frac{dv}{dx}\,dx = uv - \int \frac{du}{dx}\,v\,dx.$$

Definite integrals

$$\int_0^{\frac{1}{2}\pi}\sin^m x\,dx = \frac{m-1}{m}\int_0^{\frac{1}{2}\pi}\sin^{m-2}x\,dx; \qquad \int_0^{\frac{1}{2}\pi}\cos^m x\,dx = \frac{m-1}{m}\int_0^{\frac{1}{2}\pi}\cos^{m-2}x\,dx;$$

$$\int_0^{\frac{1}{2}\pi}\sin^m x\cos^n x\,dx = \frac{m-1}{m+n}\int_0^{\frac{1}{2}\pi}\sin^{m-2}x\cos^n x\,dx = \frac{n-1}{m+n}\int_0^{\frac{1}{2}\pi}\sin^m x\cos^{n-2}x\,dx.$$

[These results hold provided that the exponents in the reduced form are greater than -1. There are analogous reduction formulae with other intervals of integration $(\tfrac{1}{2}k_1\pi, \tfrac{1}{2}k_2\pi)$ with k_1, k_2 integral.]

DEFINITIONS AND FORMULAE

Electricity

Resistance. When a potential difference of V volts is applied across a resistor of resistance R ohms, the current flowing is I amperes, where

$$V = IR,$$

and the power consumed is P watts, where

$$P = VI = I^2R = V^2/R.$$

Capacitance. When a capacitor of capacitance C farads is charged to a potential difference of V volts, the charge on its positive plates is Q coulombs, where

$$Q = CV.$$

The energy stored in the capacitor in joules is

$$\tfrac{1}{2}QV = \tfrac{1}{2}CV^2 = \tfrac{1}{2}Q^2/C.$$

Inductance. When a variable current flows through an inductor of inductance L henries, the e.m.f. induced (which is negative if the current is increasing) is given by

$$V = -L\frac{dI}{dt}.$$

The L, C, R circuit.

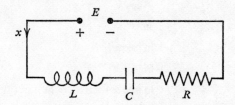

The current x and the charge Q on the capacitor satisfy the differential equation

$$L\frac{dx}{dt} + \frac{Q}{C} + Rx = E,$$

where

$$x = \frac{dQ}{dt}.$$

If E is represented by the real part of function $t \to E_0 e^{jpt}$, then x is represented by the real part of

$$t \to E_0 e^{jpt}/Z,$$

where

$$Z = R + jpL + \frac{1}{jpC} \quad \text{(the *impedance*).}$$

Mechanics

Centres of mass (uniform bodies)

Solid hemisphere	$\tfrac{3}{8}r$ from centre.
Hemispherical shell	$\tfrac{1}{2}r$ from centre.
Solid cone or pyramid	$\tfrac{1}{4}h$ above base, on line from vertex to c.m. of base (as a lamina).
Triangular lamina	At centroid.
Sector of circular lamina	$\tfrac{2}{3}r \sin\theta/\theta$ from centre, where 2θ is angle subtended at centre.
Arc of circle	$r \sin\theta/\theta$ from centre, where 2θ is angle subtended at centre.

DEFINITIONS AND FORMULAE

Moments of inertia (uniform bodies of mass m)

Rod, length l, about perpendicular axis through centre:
Rectangular lamina about axis in plane bisecting sides of length l: $\left.\right\}$ $\frac{1}{12}ml^2$

Rod, length l, about perpendicular axis through end:
Rectangular lamina about edge perpendicular to edges of length l: $\left.\right\}$ $\frac{1}{3}ml^2$

Rectangular lamina, sides l_1 and l_2, about perpendicular axis through centre: $\frac{1}{12}m(l_1^2+l_2^2)$

Hoop, radius r, about perpendicular axis through centre:
Cylindrical shell, radius r, about axis of rotational symmetry: $\left.\right\}$ mr^2

Hoop, radius r, about diameter: $\frac{1}{2}mr^2$

Disc, radius r, about perpendicular axis through centre:
Solid cylinder, radius r, about axis of rotational symmetry: $\left.\right\}$ $\frac{1}{2}mr^2$

Disc, radius r, about diameter: $\frac{1}{4}mr^2$

Solid sphere, radius r, about diameter: $\frac{2}{5}mr^2$

Spherical shell, radius r, about diameter: $\frac{2}{3}mr^2$

The *parallel axes rule*: $I_A = I_G+m.(GA)^2$.

The *perpendicular axes rule*: For a *lamina*, $I_3 = I_1+I_2$, where I_1, I_2 are moments of inertia about two axes in the plane at right angles and I_3 is the moment of inertia about the axis perpendicular to the plane through their intersection.

Expressions for velocity and acceleration in two dimensions

$\hat{\imath}, \hat{\jmath}; \hat{r}, \hat{u}; \hat{t}, \hat{n}$ are unit vectors.

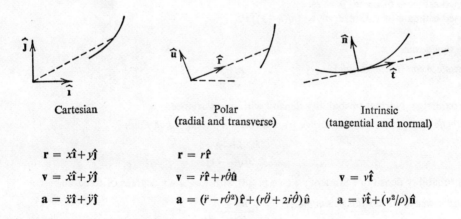

Cartesian	Polar (radial and transverse)	Intrinsic (tangential and normal)
$\mathbf{r} = x\hat{\imath}+y\hat{\jmath}$	$\mathbf{r} = r\hat{r}$	
$\mathbf{v} = \dot{x}\hat{\imath}+\dot{y}\hat{\jmath}$	$\mathbf{v} = \dot{r}\hat{r}+r\dot{\theta}\hat{u}$	$\mathbf{v} = v\hat{t}$
$\mathbf{a} = \ddot{x}\hat{\imath}+\ddot{y}\hat{\jmath}$	$\mathbf{a} = (\ddot{r}-r\dot{\theta}^2)\hat{r}+(r\ddot{\theta}+2\dot{r}\dot{\theta})\hat{u}$	$\mathbf{a} = \dot{v}\hat{t}+(v^2/\rho)\hat{n}$

Notes (i) The transverse component of acceleration in polar form can be written as $\dfrac{1}{r}\dfrac{d}{dt}(r^2\dot{\theta})$.

(ii) For motion in a circle (centre the origin) the components of acceleration in polar form are

$$-r\dot{\theta}^2 = -v^2/r \quad \text{and} \quad r\dot{\theta} = \dot{v}.$$

Motion with constant acceleration $\mathbf{a}$

$$\mathbf{v} = \mathbf{u}+t\mathbf{a}; \qquad v^2 = u^2+2\mathbf{a}.\mathbf{r};$$
$$\mathbf{r} = t\mathbf{u}+\tfrac{1}{2}t^2\mathbf{a}; \qquad \mathbf{r} = \tfrac{1}{2}t(\mathbf{u}+\mathbf{v});$$

where $\mathbf{u}$ is the value of $\mathbf{v}$ when $t = 0$, and the position at $t = 0$ is taken as origin.

DEFINITIONS AND FORMULAE

Statistics

Statistical measures

If n is the sample size and $f(x_i)$ the frequency of occurrence of the value x_i in the sample (so that $n = \Sigma f(x_i)$), then we define:

Mean

$$m(\text{or } \bar{x}) = \frac{1}{n} \sum_i x_i f(x_i).$$

Variance†

$$s^2 = \frac{1}{n} \sum_i (x_i - m)^2 f(x_i) = \frac{1}{n} \sum_i x_i^2 f(x_i) - m^2.$$

Standard deviation. s is the square root of the variance.

Correlation coefficient (product moment).

$$r = \frac{\dfrac{1}{n} \sum_i \sum_j (x_i - \bar{x})(y_j - \bar{y}) f(x_i, y_j)}{s_x s_y} = \frac{\dfrac{1}{n} \sum_i \sum_j x_i y_j f(x_i, y_j) - \bar{x}\bar{y}}{s_x s_y}.$$

Kendall's rank correlation coefficient. If the orders of all possible pairs in the two rankings are compared, the coefficient is defined as

$$\tau = \frac{\text{number of agreements} - \text{number of disagreements}}{\frac{1}{2}n(n-1)}.$$

Estimation of population parameters

If the parent population has mean μ and standard deviation σ, the sample means constitute a population with mean μ and standard deviation $\sigma/\sqrt{n}$ of approximately Normal form (for large n); and the sample variances constitute a population with mean $\{(n-1)/n\}\sigma^2$.

Unbiased estimate of mean, $\hat{\mu} = m$.

Unbiased estimate of variance, $\hat{\sigma}^2 = \{n/(n-1)\}s^2$.

Tests for significance

(i) *Sample mean (large sample).*
$$\frac{m - \mu}{s/\sqrt{n}}$$

has approximately Normal probability density with unit variance.

(ii) *Sample mean (small sample drawn from a Normal parent population).*

$$\frac{m - \mu}{s/\sqrt{(n-1)}}$$

has the probability density of Student's t (see p. 48) with $\nu = n-1$ degrees of freedom.

(iii) *Difference of means (large samples).*
$$\frac{m_1 - m_2}{\sqrt{\left\{\dfrac{s_1^2}{n_1} + \dfrac{s_2^2}{n_2}\right\}}}$$

has approximately Normal probability density with unit variance.

(iv) *Correlation coefficient (product moment).*

If
$$z = \frac{1}{2}\ln\frac{1+r}{1-r},$$

then $z\sqrt{(n-3)}$ has approximately Normal probability density with unit variance.

† Some statisticians prefer to define the sample variance differently, with a factor $1/(n-1)$ in place of $1/n$. If this convention is followed, other results involving the statistic s will, of course, take a different form from those given in these tables.

[14]

(v) *Kendall's rank correlation coefficient.*

For $n > 10$,

$$\tau \sqrt{\frac{9n(n-1)}{2(2n+5)}}$$

has approximately Normal probability density with unit variance.

(vi) *Goodness of fit.*

$$\sum \frac{\{f_e(x_i) - f_o(x_i)\}^2}{f_e(x_i)}$$

has approximately χ^2 probability density (see p. 47) for the appropriate number of degrees of freedom.

Probability

Parameters

	Discrete model	Continuous model
Mean $\mu = E[x]$	$\Sigma x_i p(x_i)$	$\int x\rho\,dx$
Variance $\sigma^2 = E[(x-\mu)^2]$	$\Sigma(x_i-\mu)^2 p(x_i)$ $= \Sigma x_i^2 p(x_i) - \mu^2$	$\int (x-\mu)^2 \rho\,dx$ $= \int x^2 \rho\,dx - \mu^2$

If $G(t)$ is a probability generator for the model,

$$\mu = G'(1); \quad \sigma^2 = G''(1) + G'(1) - \{G'(1)\}^2.$$

Particular probability models

Binomial probability function. If the probabilities of success and of failure in a single trial are a, b (where $a+b = 1$), the probability of i successes in n trials is

$$\binom{n}{i} b^{n-i} a^i.$$

Probability generator $G(t) = (b+at)^n$.
Mean $= na$; variance $= nab$.

Poisson probability function. The probability of i successes is

$$\frac{\mu^i}{i!} e^{-\mu}.$$

Probability generator $G(t) = e^{-\mu}e^{\mu t}$.
Mean $= \mu$; variance $= \mu$.

Normal probability density function. The probability density is

$$\rho = \frac{1}{\sigma} \phi\left(\frac{x-\mu}{\sigma}\right),$$

where

$$\phi(x) = \frac{1}{\sqrt{(2\pi)}} e^{-\frac{1}{2}x^2}.$$

Mean $= \mu$; variance $= \sigma^2$.

	0	1	2	3	4	5	6	7	8	9	1	2	3	4	5	6	7	8	9
1·0	·0000	0043	0086	0128	0170	0212	0253	0294	0334	0374	4	8	12	17	21	25	29	33	37
1·1	·0414	0453	0492	0531	0569	0607	0645	0682	0719	0755	4	8	11	15	19	23	27	30	34
1·2	·0792	0828	0864	0899	0934	0969	1004	1038	1072	1106	3	7	10	14	17	21	24	28	31
1·3	·1139	1173	1206	1239	1271	1303	1335	1367	1399	1430	3	6	10	13	16	19	23	26	29
1·4	·1461	1492	1523	1553	1584	1614	1644	1673	1703	1732	3	6	9	12	15	18	21	24	27
1·5	·1761	1790	1818	1847	1875	1903	1931	1959	1987	2014	3	6	8	11	14	17	20	22	25
1·6	·2041	2068	2095	2122	2148	2175	2201	2227	2253	2279	3	5	8	11	13	16	18	21	24
1·7	·2304	2330	2355	2380	2405	2430	2455	2480	2504	2529	2	5	7	10	12	15	17	20	22
1·8	·2553	2577	2601	2625	2648	2672	2695	2718	2742	2765	2	5	7	9	12	14	16	19	21
1·9	·2788	2810	2833	2856	2878	2900	2923	2945	2967	2989	2	4	7	9	11	13	16	18	20
2·0	·3010	3032	3054	3075	3096	3118	3139	3160	3181	3201	2	4	6	8	11	13	15	17	19
2·1	·3222	3243	3263	3284	3304	3324	3345	3365	3385	3404	2	4	6	8	10	12	14	16	18
2·2	·3424	3444	3464	3483	3502	3522	3541	3560	3579	3598	2	4	6	8	10	12	14	15	17
2·3	·3617	3636	3655	3674	3692	3711	3729	3747	3766	3784	2	4	6	7	9	11	13	15	17
2·4	·3802	3820	3838	3856	3874	3892	3909	3927	3945	3962	2	4	5	7	9	11	12	14	16
2·5	·3979	3997	4014	4031	4048	4065	4082	4099	4116	4133	2	3	5	7	9	10	12	14	15
2·6	·4150	4166	4183	4200	4216	4232	4249	4265	4281	4298	2	3	5	7	8	10	11	13	15
2·7	·4314	4330	4346	4362	4378	4393	4409	4425	4440	4456	2	3	5	6	8	9	11	13	14
2·8	·4472	4487	4502	4518	4533	4548	4564	4579	4594	4609	2	3	5	6	8	9	11	12	14
2·9	·4624	4639	4654	4669	4683	4698	4713	4728	4742	4757	1	3	4	6	7	9	10	12	13
3·0	·4771	4786	4800	4814	4829	4843	4857	4871	4886	4900	1	3	4	6	7	9	10	11	13
3·1	·4914	4928	4942	4955	4969	4983	4997	5011	5024	5038	1	3	4	6	7	8	10	11	12
3·2	·5051	5065	5079	5092	5105	5119	5132	5145	5159	5172	1	3	4	5	7	8	9	11	12
3·3	·5185	5198	5211	5224	5237	5250	5263	5276	5289	5302	1	3	4	5	6	8	9	10	12
3·4	·5315	5328	5340	5353	5366	5378	5391	5403	5416	5428	1	3	4	5	6	8	9	10	11
3·5	·5441	5453	5465	5478	5490	5502	5514	5527	5539	5551	1	2	4	5	6	7	9	10	11
3·6	·5563	5575	5587	5599	5611	5623	5635	5647	5658	5670	1	2	4	5	6	7	8	10	11
3·7	·5682	5694	5705	5717	5729	5740	5752	5763	5775	5786	1	2	3	5	6	7	8	9	10
3·8	·5798	5809	5821	5832	5843	5855	5866	5877	5888	5899	1	2	3	5	6	7	8	9	10
3·9	·5911	5922	5933	5944	5955	5966	5977	5988	5999	6010	1	2	3	4	6	7	8	9	10
4·0	·6021	6031	6042	6053	6064	6075	6085	6096	6107	6117	1	2	3	4	5	6	8	9	10
4·1	·6128	6138	6149	6160	6170	6180	6191	6201	6212	6222	1	2	3	4	5	6	7	8	9
4·2	·6232	6243	6253	6263	6274	6284	6294	6304	6314	6325	1	2	3	4	5	6	7	8	9
4·3	·6335	6345	6355	6365	6375	6385	6395	6405	6415	6425	1	2	3	4	5	6	7	8	9
4·4	·6435	6444	6454	6464	6474	6484	6493	6503	6513	6522	1	2	3	4	5	6	7	8	9
4·5	·6532	6542	6551	6561	6571	6580	6590	6599	6609	6618	1	2	3	4	5	6	7	8	9
4·6	·6628	6637	6646	6656	6665	6675	6684	6693	6702	6712	1	2	3	4	5	6	7	7	8
4·7	·6721	6730	6739	6749	6758	6767	6776	6785	6794	6803	1	2	3	4	5	5	6	7	8
4·8	·6812	6821	6830	6839	6848	6857	6866	6875	6884	6893	1	2	3	4	4	5	6	7	8
4·9	·6902	6911	6920	6928	6937	6946	6955	6964	6972	6981	1	2	3	4	4	5	6	7	8
5·0	·6990	6998	7007	7016	7024	7033	7042	7050	7059	7067	1	2	3	3	4	5	6	7	8
5·1	·7076	7084	7093	7101	7110	7118	7126	7135	7143	7152	1	2	3	3	4	5	6	7	8
5·2	·7160	7168	7177	7185	7193	7202	7210	7218	7226	7235	1	2	2	3	4	5	6	7	7
5·3	·7243	7251	7259	7267	7275	7284	7292	7300	7308	7316	1	2	2	3	4	5	6	7	7
	0	1	2	3	4	5	6	7	8	9	1	2	3	4	5	6	7	8	9

LOGARITHMS, BASE 10

	0	1	2	3	4	5	6	7	8	9	1	2	3	4	5	6	7	8	9
5·4	·7324	7332	7340	7348	7356	7364	7372	7380	7388	7396	1	2	2	3	4	5	6	6	7
5·5	·7404	7412	7419	7427	7435	7443	7451	7459	7466	7474	1	2	2	3	4	5	5	6	7
5·6	·7482	7490	7497	7505	7513	7520	7528	7536	7543	7551	1	2	2	3	4	5	5	6	7
5·7	·7559	7566	7574	7582	7589	7597	7604	7612	7619	7627	1	2	2	3	4	5	5	6	7
5·8	·7634	7642	7649	7657	7664	7672	7679	7686	7694	7701	1	1	2	3	4	4	5	6	7
5·9	·7709	7716	7723	7731	7738	7745	7752	7760	7767	7774	1	1	2	3	4	4	5	6	7
6·0	·7782	7789	7796	7803	7810	7818	7825	7832	7839	7846	1	1	2	3	4	4	5	6	6
6·1	·7853	7860	7868	7875	7882	7889	7896	7903	7910	7917	1	1	2	3	4	4	5	6	6
6·2	·7924	7931	7938	7945	7952	7959	7966	7973	7980	7987	1	1	2	3	3	4	5	6	6
6·3	·7993	8000	8007	8014	8021	8028	8035	8041	8048	8055	1	1	2	3	3	4	5	5	6
6·4	·8062	8069	8075	8082	8089	8096	8102	8109	8116	8122	1	1	2	3	3	4	5	5	6
6·5	·8129	8136	8142	8149	8156	8162	8169	8176	8182	8189	1	1	2	3	3	4	5	5	6
6·6	·8195	8202	8209	8215	8222	8228	8235	8241	8248	8254	1	1	2	3	3	4	5	5	6
6·7	·8261	8267	8274	8280	8287	8293	8299	8306	8312	8319	1	1	2	3	3	4	5	5	6
6·8	·8325	8331	8338	8344	8351	8357	8363	8370	8376	8382	1	1	2	3	3	4	4	5	6
6·9	·8388	8395	8401	8407	8414	8420	8426	8432	8439	8445	1	1	2	3	3	4	4	5	6
7·0	·8451	8457	8463	8470	8476	8482	8488	8494	8500	8506	1	1	2	2	3	4	4	5	6
7·1	·8513	8519	8525	8531	8537	8543	8549	8555	8561	8567	1	1	2	2	3	4	4	5	5
7·2	·8573	8579	8585	8591	8597	8603	8609	8615	8621	8627	1	1	2	2	3	4	4	5	5
7·3	·8633	8639	8645	8651	8657	8663	8669	8675	8681	8686	1	1	2	2	3	4	4	5	5
7·4	·8692	8698	8704	8710	8716	8722	8727	8733	8739	8745	1	1	2	2	3	4	4	5	5
7·5	·8751	8756	8762	8768	8774	8779	8785	8791	8797	8802	1	1	2	2	3	3	4	5	5
7·6	·8808	8814	8820	8825	8831	8837	8842	8848	8854	8859	1	1	2	2	3	3	4	5	5
7·7	·8865	8871	8876	8882	8887	8893	8899	8904	8910	8915	1	1	2	2	3	3	4	4	5
7·8	·8921	8927	8932	8938	8943	8949	8954	8960	8965	8971	1	1	2	2	3	3	4	4	5
7·9	·8976	8982	8987	8993	8998	9004	9009	9015	9020	9025	1	1	2	2	3	3	4	4	5
8·0	·9031	9036	9042	9047	9053	9058	9063	9069	9074	9079	1	1	2	2	3	3	4	4	5
8·1	·9085	9090	9096	9101	9106	9112	9117	9122	9128	9133	1	1	2	2	3	3	4	4	5
8·2	·9138	9143	9149	9154	9159	9165	9170	9175	9180	9186	1	1	2	2	3	3	4	4	5
8·3	·9191	9196	9201	9206	9212	9217	9222	9227	9232	9238	1	1	2	2	3	3	4	4	5
8·4	·9243	9248	9253	9258	9263	9269	9274	9279	9284	9289	1	1	2	2	3	3	4	4	5
8·5	·9294	9299	9304	9309	9315	9320	9325	9330	9335	9340	1	1	2	2	3	3	4	4	5
8·6	·9345	9350	9355	9360	9365	9370	9375	9380	9385	9390	1	1	2	2	3	3	4	4	5
8·7	·9395	9400	9405	9410	9415	9420	9425	9430	9435	9440	0	1	1	2	2	3	3	4	4
8·8	·9445	9450	9455	9460	9465	9469	9474	9479	9484	9489	0	1	1	2	2	3	3	4	4
8·9	·9494	9499	9504	9509	9513	9518	9523	9528	9533	9538	0	1	1	2	2	3	3	4	4
9·0	·9542	9547	9552	9557	9562	9566	9571	9576	9581	9586	0	1	1	2	2	3	3	4	4
9·1	·9590	9595	9600	9605	9609	9614	9619	9624	9628	9633	0	1	1	2	2	3	3	4	4
9·2	·9638	9643	9647	9652	9657	9661	9666	9671	9675	9680	0	1	1	2	2	3	3	4	4
9·3	·9685	9689	9694	9699	9703	9708	9713	9717	9722	9727	0	1	1	2	2	3	3	4	4
9·4	·9731	9736	9741	9745	9750	9754	9759	9763	9768	9773	0	1	1	2	2	3	3	4	4
9·5	·9777	9782	9786	9791	9795	9800	9805	9809	9814	9818	0	1	1	2	2	3	3	4	4
9·6	·9823	9827	9832	9836	9841	9845	9850	9854	9859	9863	0	1	1	2	2	3	3	4	4
9·7	·9868	9872	9877	9881	9886	9890	9894	9899	9903	9908	0	1	1	2	2	3	3	4	4
9·8	·9912	9917	9921	9926	9930	9934	9939	9943	9948	9952	0	1	1	2	2	3	3	4	4
9·9	·9956	9961	9965	9969	9974	9978	9983	9987	9991	9996	0	1	1	2	2	3	3	3	4
	0	1	2	3	4	5	6	7	8	9	1	2	3	4	5	6	7	8	9

LOGARITHMS OF SINES

	·0	·1	·2	·3	·4	·5	·6	·7	·8	·9	1·0		1	2	3	4	5	6	7	8	9
0°		3̄·242	3̄·543	3̄·719	3̄·844	3̄·941	2̄·020	2̄·087	2̄·145	2̄·196	2̄·242	89°									
1	2̄·2419	2832	3210	3558	3880	4179	4459	4723	4971	5206	5428	88									
2	2̄·5428	5640	5842	6035	6220	6397	6567	6731	6889	7041	7188	87									
3	2̄·7188	7330	7468	7602	7731	7857	7979	8098	8213	8326	8436	86									
4	2̄·8436	8543	8647	8749	8849	8946	9042	9135	9226	9315	9403	85									
5	2̄·9403	9489	9573	9655	9736	9816	9894	9970	0046	0120	0192	84									
6	1̄·0192	0264	0334	0403	0472	0539	0605	0670	0734	0797	0859	83	Use								
7	1̄·0859	0920	0981	1040	1099	1157	1214	1271	1326	1381	1436	82	Linear								
8	1̄·1436	1489	1542	1594	1646	1697	1747	1797	1847	1895	1943	81	Interpolation								
9	1̄·1943	1991	2038	2085	2131	2176	2221	2266	2310	2353	2397	80									
10	1̄·2397	2439	2482	2524	2565	2606	2647	2687	2727	2767	2806	79									
11	1̄·2806	2845	2883	2921	2959	2997	3034	3070	3107	3143	3179	78	4	7	11	15	19	22	26	30	34
12	1̄·3179	3214	3250	3284	3319	3353	3387	3421	3455	3488	3521	77	3	7	10	14	17	21	24	27	31
13	1̄·3521	3554	3586	3618	3650	3682	3713	3745	3775	3806	3837	76	3	6	9	13	16	19	22	25	28
14	1̄·3837	3867	3897	3927	3957	3986	4015	4044	4073	4102	4130	75	3	6	9	12	15	18	21	23	26
15	1̄·4130	4158	4186	4214	4242	4269	4296	4323	4350	4377	4403	74	3	5	8	11	14	16	19	22	25
16	1̄·4403	4430	4456	4482	4508	4533	4559	4584	4609	4634	4659	73	3	5	8	10	13	15	18	20	23
17	1̄·4659	4684	4709	4733	4757	4781	4805	4829	4853	4876	4900	72	2	5	7	10	12	14	17	19	22
18	1̄·4900	4923	4946	4969	4992	5015	5037	5060	5082	5104	5126	71	2	5	7	9	11	14	16	18	20
19	1̄·5126	5148	5170	5192	5213	5235	5256	5278	5299	5320	5341	70	2	4	6	9	11	13	15	17	19
20	1̄·5341	5361	5382	5402	5423	5443	5463	5484	5504	5523	5543	69	2	4	6	8	10	12	14	16	18
21	1̄·5543	5563	5583	5602	5621	5641	5660	5679	5698	5717	5736	68	2	4	6	8	10	12	13	15	17
22	1̄·5736	5754	5773	5792	5810	5828	5847	5865	5883	5901	5919	67	2	4	5	7	9	11	13	15	16
23	1̄·5919	5937	5954	5972	5990	6007	6024	6042	6059	6076	6093	66	2	3	5	7	9	10	12	14	16
24	1̄·6093	6110	6127	6144	6161	6177	6194	6210	6227	6243	6259	65	2	3	5	7	8	10	12	13	15
25	1̄·6259	6276	6292	6308	6324	6340	6356	6371	6387	6403	6418	64	2	3	5	6	8	10	11	13	14
26	1̄·6418	6434	6449	6465	6480	6495	6510	6526	6541	6556	6570	63	2	3	5	6	8	9	11	12	14
27	1̄·6570	6585	6600	6615	6629	6644	6659	6673	6687	6702	6716	62	1	3	4	6	7	9	10	12	13
28	1̄·6716	6730	6744	6759	6773	6787	6801	6814	6828	6842	6856	61	1	3	4	6	7	8	10	11	13
29	1̄·6856	6869	6883	6896	6910	6923	6937	6950	6963	6977	6990	60	1	3	4	5	7	8	9	11	12
30	1̄·6990	7003	7016	7029	7042	7055	7068	7080	7093	7106	7118	59	1	3	4	5	6	8	9	10	12
31	1̄·7118	7131	7144	7156	7168	7181	7193	7205	7218	7230	7242	58	1	2	4	5	6	7	9	10	11
32	1̄·7242	7254	7266	7278	7290	7302	7314	7326	7338	7349	7361	57	1	2	4	5	6	7	8	10	11
33	1̄·7361	7373	7384	7396	7407	7419	7430	7442	7453	7464	7476	56	1	2	3	5	6	7	8	9	10
34	1̄·7476	7487	7498	7509	7520	7531	7542	7553	7564	7575	7586	55	1	2	3	4	6	7	8	9	10
35	1̄·7586	7597	7607	7618	7629	7640	7650	7661	7671	7682	7692	54	1	2	3	4	5	6	7	9	10
36	1̄·7692	7703	7713	7723	7734	7744	7754	7764	7774	7785	7795	53	1	2	3	4	5	6	7	8	9
37	1̄·7795	7805	7815	7825	7835	7844	7854	7864	7874	7884	7893	52	1	2	3	4	5	6	7	8	9
38	1̄·7893	7903	7913	7922	7932	7941	7951	7960	7970	7979	7989	51	1	2	3	4	5	6	7	8	9
39	1̄·7989	7998	8007	8017	8026	8035	8044	8053	8063	8072	8081	50	1	2	3	4	5	6	6	7	8
40	1̄·8081	8090	8099	8108	8117	8125	8134	8143	8152	8161	8169	49	1	2	3	4	4	5	6	7	8
41	1̄·8169	8178	8187	8195	8204	8213	8221	8230	8238	8247	8255	48	1	2	3	3	4	5	6	7	8
42	1̄·8255	8264	8272	8280	8289	8297	8305	8313	8322	8330	8338	47	1	2	2	3	4	5	6	7	7
43	1̄·8338	8346	8354	8362	8370	8378	8386	8394	8402	8410	8418	46	1	2	2	3	4	5	6	6	7
	1·0	·9	·8	·7	·6	·5	·4	·3	·2	·1	·0		1	2	3	4	5	6	7	8	9

LOGARITHMS OF COSINES

	·0	·1	·2	·3	·4	·5	·6	·7	·8	·9	1·0		1	2	3	4	5	6	7	8	9
44°	Ī·8418	8426	8433	8441	8449	8457	8464	8472	8480	8487	8495	45°	1	2	2	3	4	5	5	6	7
45	Ī·8495	8502	8510	8517	8525	8532	8540	8547	8555	8562	8569	44	1	1	2	3	4	4	5	6	7
46	Ī·8569	8577	8584	8591	8598	8606	8613	8620	8627	8634	8641	43	1	1	2	3	4	4	5	6	6
47	Ī·8641	8648	8655	8662	8669	8676	8683	8690	8697	8704	8711	42	1	1	2	3	3	4	5	6	6
48	Ī·8711	8718	8724	8731	8738	8745	8751	8758	8765	8771	8778	41	1	1	2	3	3	4	5	5	6
49	Ī·8778	8784	8791	8797	8804	8810	8817	8823	8830	8836	8843	40	1	1	2	3	3	4	5	5	6
50	Ī·8843	8849	8855	8862	8868	8874	8880	8887	8893	8899	8905	39	1	1	2	2	3	4	4	5	6
51	Ī·8905	8911	8917	8923	8929	8935	8941	8947	8953	8959	8965	38	1	1	2	2	3	4	4	5	5
52	Ī·8965	8971	8977	8983	8989	8995	9000	9006	9012	9018	9023	37	1	1	2	2	3	3	4	5	5
53	Ī·9023	9029	9035	9041	9046	9052	9057	9063	9069	9074	9080	36	1	1	2	2	3	3	4	4	5
54	Ī·9080	9085	9091	9096	9101	9107	9112	9118	9123	9128	9134	35	1	1	2	2	3	3	4	4	5
55	Ī·9134	9139	9144	9149	9155	9160	9165	9170	9175	9181	9186	34	1	1	2	2	3	3	4	4	5
56	Ī·9186	9191	9196	9201	9206	9211	9216	9221	9226	9231	9236	33	1	1	2	2	3	3	4	4	5
57	Ī·9236	9241	9246	9251	9255	9260	9265	9270	9275	9279	9284	32	0	1	1	2	2	3	3	4	4
58	Ī·9284	9289	9294	9298	9303	9308	9312	9317	9322	9326	9331	31	0	1	1	2	2	3	3	4	4
59	Ī·9331	9335	9340	9344	9349	9353	9358	9362	9367	9371	9375	30	0	1	1	2	2	3	3	4	4
60	Ī·9375	9380	9384	9388	9393	9397	9401	9406	9410	9414	9418	29	0	1	1	2	2	3	3	3	4
61	Ī·9418	9422	9427	9431	9435	9439	9443	9447	9451	9455	9459	28	0	1	1	2	2	2	3	3	4
62	Ī·9459	9463	9467	9471	9475	9479	9483	9487	9491	9495	9499	27	0	1	1	2	2	2	3	3	4
63	Ī·9499	9503	9506	9510	9514	9518	9522	9525	9529	9533	9537	26	0	1	1	2	2	2	3	3	3
64	Ī·9537	9540	9544	9548	9551	9555	9558	9562	9566	9569	9573	25	0	1	1	1	2	2	3	3	3
65	Ī·9573	9576	9580	9583	9587	9590	9594	9597	9601	9604	9607	24	0	1	1	1	2	2	2	3	3
66	Ī·9607	9611	9614	9617	9621	9624	9627	9631	9634	9637	9640	23	0	1	1	1	2	2	2	3	3
67	Ī·9640	9643	9647	9650	9653	9656	9659	9662	9666	9669	9672	22	0	1	1	1	2	2	2	3	3
68	Ī·9672	9675	9678	9681	9684	9687	9690	9693	9696	9699	9702	21	0	1	1	1	1	2	2	2	3
69	Ī·9702	9704	9707	9710	9713	9716	9719	9722	9724	9727	9730	20	0	1	1	1	1	2	2	2	3
70	Ī·9730	9733	9735	9738	9741	9743	9746	9749	9751	9754	9757	19	0	1	1	1	1	2	2	2	2
71	Ī·9757	9759	9762	9764	9767	9770	9772	9775	9777	9780	9782	18	0	1	1	1	1	2	2	2	2
72	Ī·9782	9785	9787	9789	9792	9794	9797	9799	9801	9804	9806	17	0	0	1	1	1	1	2	2	2
73	Ī·9806	9808	9811	9813	9815	9817	9820	9822	9824	9826	9828	16	0	0	1	1	1	1	2	2	2
74	Ī·9828	9831	9833	9835	9837	9839	9841	9843	9845	9847	9849	15	0	0	1	1	1	1	1	2	2
75	Ī·9849	9851	9853	9855	9857	9859	9861	9863	9865	9867	9869	14	0	0	1	1	1	1	1	2	2
76	Ī·9869	9871	9873	9875	9876	9878	9880	9882	9884	9885	9887	13	0	0	1	1	1	1	1	1	2
77	Ī·9887	9889	9891	9892	9894	9896	9897	9899	9901	9902	9904	12	0	0	1	1	1	1	1	1	2
78	Ī·9904	9906	9907	9909	9910	9912	9913	9915	9916	9918	9919	11	0	0	0	1	1	1	1	1	1
79	Ī·9919	9921	9922	9924	9925	9927	9928	9929	9931	9932	9934	10	0	0	0	1	1	1	1	1	1
80	Ī·9934	9935	9936	9937	9939	9940	9941	9943	9944	9945	9946	9	0	0	0	1	1	1	1	1	1
81	Ī·9946	9947	9949	9950	9951	9952	9953	9954	9955	9956	9958	8	0	0	0	0	1	1	1	1	1
82	Ī·9958	9959	9960	9961	9962	9963	9964	9965	9966	9967	9968	7	0	0	0	0	0	1	1	1	1
83	Ī·9968	9968	9969	9970	9971	9972	9973	9974	9975	9975	9976	6									
84	Ī·9976	9977	9978	9978	9979	9980	9981	9981	9982	9983	9983	5									
85	Ī·9983	9984	9985	9985	9986	9987	9987	9988	9988	9989	9989	4									
86	Ī·9989	9990	9990	9991	9991	9992	9992	9993	9993	9994	9994	3									
87	Ī·9994	9994	9995	9995	9996	9996	9996	9996	9997	9997	9997	2									
88	Ī·9997	9998	9998	9998	9998	9999	9999	9999	9999	9999	9999	1									
89	Ī·9999	9999	0000	0000	0000	0000	0000	0000	0000	0000	0000	0									
	1·0	·9	·8	·7	·6	·5	·4	·3	·2	·1	·0		1	2	3	4	5	6	7	8	9

LOGARITHMS OF COSINES

LOGARITHMS OF TANGENTS

	·0	·1	·2	·3	·4	·5	·6	·7	·8	·9	1·0		1 2 3 4 5 6 7 8 9
0°		$\bar{3}$·242	$\bar{3}$·543	$\bar{3}$·719	$\bar{3}$·844	$\bar{3}$·941	$\bar{2}$·020	$\bar{2}$·087	$\bar{2}$·145	$\bar{2}$·196	$\bar{2}$·242	89°	
1	$\bar{2}$·2419	2833	3211	3559	3881	4181	4461	4725	4973	5208	5431	88	
2	$\bar{2}$·5431	5643	5845	6038	6223	6401	6571	6736	6894	7046	7194	87	
3	$\bar{2}$·7194	7337	7475	7609	7739	7865	7988	8107	8223	8336	8446	86	
4	$\bar{2}$·8446	8554	8659	8762	8862	8960	9056	9150	9241	9331	9420	85	
5	$\bar{2}$·9420	9506	9591	9674	9756	9836	9915	9992	0068	0143	0216	84	Use
6	$\bar{1}$·0216	0289	0360	0430	0499	0567	0633	0699	0764	0828	0891	83	Linear
7	$\bar{1}$·0891	0954	1015	1076	1135	1194	1252	1310	1367	1423	1478	82	Interpolation
8	$\bar{1}$·1478	1533	1587	1640	1693	1745	1797	1848	1898	1948	1997	81	
9	$\bar{1}$·1997	2046	2094	2142	2189	2236	2282	2328	2374	2419	2463	80	
10	$\bar{1}$·2463	2507	2551	2594	2637	2680	2722	2764	2805	2846	2887	79	
11	$\bar{1}$·2887	2927	2967	3006	3046	3085	3123	3162	3200	3237	3275	78	4 8 12 16 19 23 27 31 35
12	$\bar{1}$·3275	3312	3349	3385	3422	3458	3493	3529	3564	3599	3634	77	4 7 11 14 18 22 25 29 32
13	$\bar{1}$·3634	3668	3702	3736	3770	3804	3837	3870	3903	3935	3968	76	3 7 10 13 17 20 23 27 30
14	$\bar{1}$·3968	4000	4032	4064	4095	4127	4158	4189	4220	4250	4281	75	3 6 9 13 16 19 22 25 28
15	$\bar{1}$·4281	4311	4341	4371	4400	4430	4459	4488	4517	4546	4575	74	3 6 9 12 15 18 21 24 26
16	$\bar{1}$·4575	4603	4632	4660	4688	4716	4744	4771	4799	4826	4853	73	3 6 8 11 14 17 19 22 25
17	$\bar{1}$·4853	4880	4907	4934	4961	4987	5014	5040	5066	5092	5118	72	3 5 8 11 13 16 19 21 24
18	$\bar{1}$·5118	5143	5169	5195	5220	5245	5270	5295	5320	5345	5370	71	3 5 8 10 13 15 18 20 23
19	$\bar{1}$·5370	5394	5419	5443	5467	5491	5516	5539	5563	5587	5611	70	2 5 7 10 12 14 17 19 22
20	$\bar{1}$·5611	5634	5658	5681	5704	5727	5750	5773	5796	5819	5842	69	2 5 7 9 12 14 16 18 21
21	$\bar{1}$·5842	5864	5887	5909	5932	5954	5976	5998	6020	6042	6064	68	2 4 7 9 11 13 16 18 20
22	$\bar{1}$·6064	6086	6108	6129	6151	6172	6194	6215	6236	6257	6279	67	2 4 6 9 11 13 15 17 19
23	$\bar{1}$·6279	6300	6321	6341	6362	6383	6404	6424	6445	6465	6486	66	2 4 6 8 10 12 15 17 19
24	$\bar{1}$·6486	6506	6527	6547	6567	6587	6607	6627	6647	6667	6687	65	2 4 6 8 10 12 14 16 18
25	$\bar{1}$·6687	6706	6726	6746	6765	6785	6804	6824	6843	6863	6882	64	2 4 6 8 10 12 14 16 18
26	$\bar{1}$·6882	6901	6920	6939	6958	6977	6996	7015	7034	7053	7072	63	2 4 6 8 9 11 13 15 17
27	$\bar{1}$·7072	7090	7109	7128	7146	7165	7183	7202	7220	7238	7257	62	2 4 6 7 9 11 13 15 17
28	$\bar{1}$·7257	7275	7293	7311	7330	7348	7366	7384	7402	7420	7438	61	2 4 5 7 9 11 13 14 16
29	$\bar{1}$·7438	7455	7473	7491	7509	7526	7544	7562	7579	7597	7614	60	2 4 5 7 9 11 12 14 16
30	$\bar{1}$·7614	7632	7649	7667	7684	7701	7719	7736	7753	7771	7788	59	2 3 5 7 9 10 12 14 16
31	$\bar{1}$·7788	7805	7822	7839	7856	7873	7890	7907	7924	7941	7958	58	2 3 5 7 9 10 12 14 15
32	$\bar{1}$·7958	7975	7992	8008	8025	8042	8059	8075	8092	8109	8125	57	2 3 5 7 8 10 12 13 15
33	$\bar{1}$·8125	8142	8158	8175	8191	8208	8224	8241	8257	8274	8290	56	2 3 5 7 8 10 12 13 15
34	$\bar{1}$·8290	8306	8323	8339	8355	8371	8388	8404	8420	8436	8452	55	2 3 5 6 8 10 11 13 15
35	$\bar{1}$·8452	8468	8484	8501	8517	8533	8549	8565	8581	8597	8613	54	2 3 5 6 8 10 11 13 14
36	$\bar{1}$·8613	8629	8644	8660	8676	8692	8708	8724	8740	8755	8771	53	2 3 5 6 8 10 11 13 14
37	$\bar{1}$·8771	8787	8803	8818	8834	8850	8865	8881	8897	8912	8928	52	2 3 5 6 8 9 11 13 14
38	$\bar{1}$·8928	8944	8959	8975	8990	9006	9022	9037	9053	9068	9084	51	2 3 5 6 8 9 11 12 14
39	$\bar{1}$·9084	9099	9115	9130	9146	9161	9176	9192	9207	9223	9238	50	2 3 5 6 8 9 11 12 14
40	$\bar{1}$·9238	9254	9269	9284	9300	9315	9330	9346	9361	9376	9392	49	2 3 5 6 8 9 11 12 14
41	$\bar{1}$·9392	9407	9422	9438	9453	9468	9483	9499	9514	9529	9544	48	2 3 5 6 8 9 11 12 14
42	$\bar{1}$·9544	9560	9575	9590	9605	9621	9636	9651	9666	9681	9697	47	2 3 5 6 8 9 11 12 14
43	$\bar{1}$·9697	9712	9727	9742	9757	9772	9788	9803	9818	9833	9848	46	2 3 5 6 8 9 11 12 14
	1·0	·9	·8	·7	·6	·5	·4	·3	·2	·1	·0		1 2 3 4 5 6 7 8 9

LOGARITHMS OF COTANGENTS

LOGARITHMS OF TANGENTS

	·0	·1	·2	·3	·4	·5	·6	·7	·8	·9	1·0		1	2	3	4	5	6	7	8	9
44°	$\overline{1}$·9848	9864	9879	9894	9909	9924	9939	9955	9970	9985	0000	45°	2	3	5	6	8	9	11	12	14
45	0·0000	0015	0030	0045	0061	0076	0091	0106	0121	0136	0152	44	2	3	5	6	8	9	11	12	14
46	0·0152	0167	0182	0197	0212	0228	0243	0258	0273	0288	0303	43	2	3	5	6	8	9	11	12	14
47	0·0303	0319	0334	0349	0364	0379	0395	0410	0425	0440	0456	42	2	3	5	6	8	9	11	12	14
48	0·0456	0471	0486	0501	0517	0532	0547	0562	0578	0593	0608	41	2	3	5	6	8	9	11	12	14
49	0·0608	0624	0639	0654	0670	0685	0700	0716	0731	0746	0762	40	2	3	5	6	8	9	11	12	14
50	0·0762	0777	0793	0808	0824	0839	0854	0870	0885	0901	0916	39	2	3	5	6	8	9	11	12	14
51	0·0916	0932	0947	0963	0978	0994	1010	1025	1041	1056	1072	38	2	3	5	6	8	9	11	12	14
52	0·1072	1088	1103	1119	1135	1150	1166	1182	1197	1213	1229	37	2	3	5	6	8	9	11	13	14
53	0·1229	1245	1260	1276	1292	1308	1324	1340	1356	1371	1387	36	2	3	5	6	8	10	11	13	14
54	0·1387	1403	1419	1435	1451	1467	1483	1499	1516	1532	1548	35	2	3	5	6	8	10	11	13	14
55	0·1548	1564	1580	1596	1612	1629	1645	1661	1677	1694	1710	34	2	3	5	6	8	10	11	13	15
56	0·1710	1726	1743	1759	1776	1792	1809	1825	1842	1858	1875	33	2	3	5	7	8	10	12	13	15
57	0·1875	1891	1908	1925	1941	1958	1975	1992	2008	2025	2042	32	2	3	5	7	8	10	12	13	15
58	0·2042	2059	2076	2093	2110	2127	2144	2161	2178	2195	2212	31	2	3	5	7	9	10	12	14	15
59	0·2212	2229	2247	2264	2281	2299	2316	2333	2351	2368	2386	30	2	3	5	7	9	10	12	14	16
60	0·2386	2403	2421	2438	2456	2474	2491	2509	2527	2545	2562	29	2	4	5	7	9	11	12	14	16
61	0·2562	2580	2598	2616	2634	2652	2670	2689	2707	2725	2743	28	2	4	5	7	9	11	13	14	16
62	0·2743	2762	2780	2798	2817	2835	2854	2872	2891	2910	2928	27	2	4	6	7	9	11	13	15	17
63	0·2928	2947	2966	2985	3004	3023	3042	3061	3080	3099	3118	26	2	4	6	8	9	11	13	15	17
64	0·3118	3137	3157	3176	3196	3215	3235	3254	3274	3294	3313	25	2	4	6	8	10	12	14	16	18
65	0·3313	3333	3353	3373	3393	3413	3433	3453	3473	3494	3514	24	2	4	6	8	10	12	14	16	18
66	0·3514	3535	3555	3576	3596	3617	3638	3659	3679	3700	3721	23	2	4	6	8	10	12	15	17	19
67	0·3721	3743	3764	3785	3806	3828	3849	3871	3892	3914	3936	22	2	4	6	9	11	13	15	17	19
68	0·3936	3958	3980	4002	4024	4046	4068	4091	4113	4136	4158	21	2	4	7	9	11	13	16	18	20
69	0·4158	4181	4204	4227	4250	4273	4296	4319	4342	4366	4389	20	2	5	7	9	12	14	16	18	21
70	0·4389	4413	4437	4461	4484	4509	4533	4557	4581	4606	4630	19	2	5	7	10	12	14	17	19	22
71	0·4630	4655	4680	4705	4730	4755	4780	4805	4831	4857	4882	18	3	5	8	10	13	15	18	20	23
72	0·4882	4908	4934	4960	4986	5013	5039	5066	5093	5120	5147	17	3	5	8	11	13	16	19	21	24
73	0·5147	5174	5201	5229	5256	5284	5312	5340	5368	5397	5425	16	3	6	8	11	14	17	19	22	25
74	0·5425	5454	5483	5512	5541	5570	5600	5629	5659	5689	5719	15	3	6	9	12	15	18	21	24	26
75	0·5719	5750	5780	5811	5842	5873	5905	5936	5968	6000	6032	14	3	6	9	13	16	19	22	25	28
76	0·6032	6065	6097	6130	6163	6196	6230	6264	6298	6332	6366	13	3	7	10	13	17	20	23	27	30
77	0·6366	6401	6436	6471	6507	6542	6578	6615	6651	6688	6725	12	4	7	11	14	18	22	25	29	32
78	0·6725	6763	6800	6838	6877	6915	6954	6994	7033	7073	7113	11	4	8	12	16	19	23	27	31	35
79	0·7113	7154	7195	7236	7278	7320	7363	7406	7449	7493	7537	10	4	8	13	17	21	25	30	34	38
80	0·7537	7581	7626	7672	7718	7764	7811	7858	7906	7954	8003	9									
81	0·8003	8052	8102	8152	8203	8255	8307	8360	8413	8467	8522	8									
82	0·8522	8577	8633	8690	8748	8806	8865	8924	8985	9046	9109	7	Use								
83	0·9109	9172	9236	9301	9367	9433	9501	9570	9640	9711	9784	6	Linear								
84	0·9784	9857	9932	0008	0085	0164	0244	0326	0409	0494	0580	5	Interpolation								
85	1·0580	0669	0759	0850	0944	1040	1138	1238	1341	1446	1554	4									
86	1·1554	1664	1777	1893	2012	2135	2261	2391	2525	2663	2806	3									
87	1·2806	2954	3106	3264	3429	3599	3777	3962	4155	4357	4569	2									
88	1·4569	4792	5027	5275	5539	5819	6119	6441	6789	7167	7581	1									
89	1·7581	8038	8550	9130	9800	2·0591	2·1561	2·2810	2·4571	2·7581		0									
	1·0	·9	·8	·7	·6	·5	·4	·3	·2	·1	·0		1	2	3	4	5	6	7	8	9

LOGARITHMS OF COTANGENTS

NATURAL SINES

	·0	·1	·2	·3	·4	·5	·6	·7	·8	·9	1·0		1	2	3	4	5	6	7	8	9
0°	·0000	0017	0035	0052	0070	0087	0105	0122	0140	0157	0175	89°	2	3	5	7	9	10	12	14	16
1	·0175	0192	0209	0227	0244	0262	0279	0297	0314	0332	0349	88	2	3	5	7	9	10	12	14	16
2	·0349	0366	0384	0401	0419	0436	0454	0471	0488	0506	0523	87	2	3	5	7	9	10	12	14	16
3	·0523	0541	0558	0576	0593	0610	0628	0645	0663	0680	0698	86	2	3	5	7	9	10	12	14	16
4	·0698	0715	0732	0750	0767	0785	0802	0819	0837	0854	0872	85	2	3	5	7	9	10	12	14	16
5	·0872	0889	0906	0924	0941	0958	0976	0993	1011	1028	1045	84	2	3	5	7	9	10	12	14	16
6	·1045	1063	1080	1097	1115	1132	1149	1167	1184	1201	1219	83	2	3	5	7	9	10	12	14	16
7	·1219	1236	1253	1271	1288	1305	1323	1340	1357	1374	1392	82	2	3	5	7	9	10	12	14	16
8	·1392	1409	1426	1444	1461	1478	1495	1513	1530	1547	1564	81	2	3	5	7	9	10	12	14	16
9	·1564	1582	1599	1616	1633	1650	1668	1685	1702	1719	1736	80	2	3	5	7	9	10	12	14	15
10	·1736	1754	1771	1788	1805	1822	1840	1857	1874	1891	1908	79	2	3	5	7	9	10	12	14	15
11	·1908	1925	1942	1959	1977	1994	2011	2028	2045	2062	2079	78	2	3	5	7	9	10	12	14	15
12	·2079	2096	2113	2130	2147	2164	2181	2198	2215	2233	2250	77	2	3	5	7	9	10	12	14	15
13	·2250	2267	2284	2300	2317	2334	2351	2368	2385	2402	2419	76	2	3	5	7	8	10	12	14	15
14	·2419	2436	2453	2470	2487	2504	2521	2538	2554	2571	2588	75	2	3	5	7	8	10	12	14	15
15	·2588	2605	2622	2639	2656	2672	2689	2706	2723	2740	2756	74	2	3	5	7	8	10	12	13	15
16	·2756	2773	2790	2807	2823	2840	2857	2874	2890	2907	2924	73	2	3	5	7	8	10	12	13	15
17	·2924	2940	2957	2974	2990	3007	3024	3040	3057	3074	3090	72	2	3	5	7	8	10	12	13	15
18	·3090	3107	3123	3140	3156	3173	3190	3206	3223	3239	3256	71	2	3	5	7	8	10	12	13	15
19	·3256	3272	3289	3305	3322	3338	3355	3371	3387	3404	3420	70	2	3	5	7	8	10	12	13	15
20	·3420	3437	3453	3469	3486	3502	3518	3535	3551	3567	3584	69	2	3	5	7	8	10	11	13	15
21	·3584	3600	3616	3633	3649	3665	3681	3697	3714	3730	3746	68	2	3	5	6	8	10	11	13	15
22	·3746	3762	3778	3795	3811	3827	3843	3859	3875	3891	3907	67	2	3	5	6	8	10	11	13	15
23	·3907	3923	3939	3955	3971	3987	4003	4019	4035	4051	4067	66	2	3	5	6	8	10	11	13	14
24	·4067	4083	4099	4115	4131	4147	4163	4179	4195	4210	4226	65	2	3	5	6	8	10	11	13	14
25	·4226	4242	4258	4274	4289	4305	4321	4337	4352	4368	4384	64	2	3	5	6	8	9	11	13	14
26	·4384	4399	4415	4431	4446	4462	4478	4493	4509	4524	4540	63	2	3	5	6	8	9	11	12	14
27	·4540	4555	4571	4586	4602	4617	4633	4648	4664	4679	4695	62	2	3	5	6	8	9	11	12	14
28	·4695	4710	4726	4741	4756	4772	4787	4802	4818	4833	4848	61	2	3	5	6	8	9	11	12	14
29	·4848	4863	4879	4894	4909	4924	4939	4955	4970	4985	5000	60	2	3	5	6	8	9	11	12	14
30	·5000	5015	5030	5045	5060	5075	5090	5105	5120	5135	5150	59	2	3	5	6	8	9	11	12	14
31	·5150	5165	5180	5195	5210	5225	5240	5255	5270	5284	5299	58	1	3	4	6	7	9	10	12	13
32	·5299	5314	5329	5344	5358	5373	5388	5402	5417	5432	5446	57	1	3	4	6	7	9	10	12	13
33	·5446	5461	5476	5490	5505	5519	5534	5548	5563	5577	5592	56	1	3	4	6	7	9	10	12	13
34	·5592	5606	5621	5635	5650	5664	5678	5693	5707	5721	5736	55	1	3	4	6	7	9	10	11	13
35	·5736	5750	5764	5779	5793	5807	5821	5835	5850	5864	5878	54	1	3	4	6	7	9	10	11	13
36	·5878	5892	5906	5920	5934	5948	5962	5976	5990	6004	6018	53	1	3	4	6	7	8	10	11	13
37	·6018	6032	6046	6060	6074	6088	6101	6115	6129	6143	6157	52	1	3	4	6	7	8	10	11	12
38	·6157	6170	6184	6198	6211	6225	6239	6252	6266	6280	6293	51	1	3	4	5	7	8	10	11	12
39	·6293	6307	6320	6334	6347	6361	6374	6388	6401	6414	6428	50	1	3	4	5	7	8	9	11	12
40	·6428	6441	6455	6468	6481	6494	6508	6521	6534	6547	6561	49	1	3	4	5	7	8	9	11	12
41	·6561	6574	6587	6600	6613	6626	6639	6652	6665	6678	6691	48	1	3	4	5	7	8	9	10	12
42	·6691	6704	6717	6730	6743	6756	6769	6782	6794	6807	6820	47	1	3	4	5	6	8	9	10	12
43	·6820	6833	6845	6858	6871	6884	6896	6909	6921	6934	6947	46	1	3	4	5	6	8	9	10	11
	1·0	·9	·8	·7	·6	·5	·4	·3	·2	·1	·0		1	2	3	4	5	6	7	8	9

NATURAL COSINES

NATURAL SINES

	·0	·1	·2	·3	·4	·5	·6	·7	·8	·9	1·0		1	2	3	4	5	6	7	8	9
44°	·6947	6959	6972	6984	6997	7009	7022	7034	7046	7059	7071	45°	1	2	4	5	6	7	9	10	11
45	·7071	7083	7096	7108	7120	7133	7145	7157	7169	7181	7193	44	1	2	4	5	6	7	9	10	11
46	·7193	7206	7218	7230	7242	7254	7266	7278	7290	7302	7314	43	1	2	4	5	6	7	8	10	11
47	·7314	7325	7337	7349	7361	7373	7385	7396	7408	7420	7431	42	1	2	4	5	6	7	8	9	11
48	·7431	7443	7455	7466	7478	7490	7501	7513	7524	7536	7547	41	1	2	3	5	6	7	8	9	10
49	·7547	7559	7570	7581	7593	7604	7615	7627	7638	7649	7660	40	1	2	3	5	6	7	8	9	10
50	·7660	7672	7683	7694	7705	7716	7727	7738	7749	7760	7771	39	1	2	3	4	6	7	8	9	10
51	·7771	7782	7793	7804	7815	7826	7837	7848	7859	7869	7880	38	1	2	3	4	5	7	8	9	10
52	·7880	7891	7902	7912	7923	7934	7944	7955	7965	7976	7986	37	1	2	3	4	5	6	7	8	10
53	·7986	7997	8007	8018	8028	8039	8049	8059	8070	8080	8090	36	1	2	3	4	5	6	7	8	9
54	·8090	8100	8111	8121	8131	8141	8151	8161	8171	8181	8192	35	1	2	3	4	5	6	7	8	9
55	·8192	8202	8211	8221	8231	8241	8251	8261	8271	8281	8290	34	1	2	3	4	5	6	7	8	9
56	·8290	8300	8310	8320	8329	8339	8348	8358	8368	8377	8387	33	1	2	3	4	5	6	7	8	9
57	·8387	8396	8406	8415	8425	8434	8443	8453	8462	8471	8480	32	1	2	3	4	5	6	7	8	8
58	·8480	8490	8499	8508	8517	8526	8536	8545	8554	8563	8572	31	1	2	3	4	5	5	6	7	8
59	·8572	8581	8590	8599	8607	8616	8625	8634	8643	8652	8660	30	1	2	3	4	4	5	6	7	8
60	·8660	8669	8678	8686	8695	8704	8712	8721	8729	8738	8746	29	1	2	3	3	4	5	6	7	8
61	·8746	8755	8763	8771	8780	8788	8796	8805	8813	8821	8829	28	1	2	2	3	4	5	6	7	7
62	·8829	8838	8846	8854	8862	8870	8878	8886	8894	8902	8910	27	1	2	2	3	4	5	6	6	7
63	·8910	8918	8926	8934	8942	8949	8957	8965	8973	8980	8988	26	1	2	2	3	4	5	5	6	7
64	·8988	8996	9003	9011	9018	9026	9033	9041	9048	9056	9063	25	1	2	2	3	4	5	5	6	7
65	·9063	9070	9078	9085	9092	9100	9107	9114	9121	9128	9135	24	1	1	2	3	4	4	5	6	7
66	·9135	9143	9150	9157	9164	9171	9178	9184	9191	9198	9205	23	1	1	2	3	3	4	5	6	6
67	·9205	9212	9219	9225	9232	9239	9245	9252	9259	9265	9272	22	1	1	2	3	3	4	5	5	6
68	·9272	9278	9285	9291	9298	9304	9311	9317	9323	9330	9336	21	1	1	2	3	3	4	4	5	6
69	·9336	9342	9348	9354	9361	9367	9373	9379	9385	9391	9397	20	1	1	2	2	3	4	4	5	6
70	·9397	9403	9409	9415	9421	9426	9432	9438	9444	9449	9455	19	1	1	2	2	3	3	4	5	5
71	·9455	9461	9466	9472	9478	9483	9489	9494	9500	9505	9511	18	1	1	2	2	3	3	4	4	5
72	·9511	9516	9521	9527	9532	9537	9542	9548	9553	9558	9563	17	1	1	2	2	3	3	4	4	5
73	·9563	9568	9573	9578	9583	9588	9593	9598	9603	9608	9613	16	0	1	1	2	2	3	3	4	4
74	·9613	9617	9622	9627	9632	9636	9641	9646	9650	9655	9659	15	0	1	1	2	2	3	3	4	4
75	·9659	9664	9668	9673	9677	9681	9686	9690	9694	9699	9703	14	0	1	1	2	2	3	3	3	4
76	·9703	9707	9711	9715	9720	9724	9728	9732	9736	9740	9744	13	0	1	1	2	2	2	3	3	4
77	·9744	9748	9751	9755	9759	9763	9767	9770	9774	9778	9781	12	0	1	1	2	2	2	3	3	3
78	·9781	9785	9789	9792	9796	9799	9803	9806	9810	9813	9816	11	0	1	1	1	2	2	2	3	3
79	·9816	9820	9823	9826	9829	9833	9836	9839	9842	9845	9848	10	0	1	1	1	2	2	2	3	3
80	·9848	9851	9854	9857	9860	9863	9866	9869	9871	9874	9877	9	0	1	1	1	1	2	2	2	3
81	·9877	9880	9882	9885	9888	9890	9893	9895	9898	9900	9903	8	0	1	1	1	1	2	2	2	2
82	·9903	9905	9907	9910	9912	9914	9917	9919	9921	9923	9925	7	0	0	1	1	1	1	2	2	2
83	·9925	9928	9930	9932	9934	9936	9938	9940	9942	9943	9945	6	0	0	1	1	1	1	1	2	2
84	·9945	9947	9949	9951	9952	9954	9956	9957	9959	9960	9962	5	0	0	1	1	1	1	1	1	2
85	·9962	9963	9965	9966	9968	9969	9971	9972	9973	9974	9976	4	0	0	0	1	1	1	1	1	1
86	·9976	9977	9978	9979	9980	9981	9982	9983	9984	9985	9986	3	0	0	0	0	1	1	1	1	1
87	·9986	9987	9988	9989	9990	9990	9991	9992	9993	9993	9994	2	0	0	0	0	0	0	1	1	1
88	·9994	9995	9995	9996	9996	9997	9997	9997	9998	9998	9998	1	0	0	0	0	0	0	0	0	0
89	·9998	9999	9999	9999	9999	0000	0000	0000	0000	0000	0000	0	0	0	0	0	0	0	0	0	0
	1·0	·9	·8	·7	·6	·5	·4	·3	·2	·1	·0		1	2	3	4	5	6	7	8	9

NATURAL COSINES

NATURAL TANGENTS

	·0	·1	·2	·3	·4	·5	·6	·7	·8	·9	1·0		1	2	3	4	5	6	7	8	9
0°	0·0000	0017	0035	0052	0070	0087	0105	0122	0140	0157	0175	89°	2	3	5	7	9	10	12	14	16
1	0·0175	0192	0209	0227	0244	0262	0279	0297	0314	0332	0349	88	2	3	5	7	9	10	12	14	16
2	0·0349	0367	0384	0402	0419	0437	0454	0472	0489	0507	0524	87	2	3	5	7	9	10	12	14	16
3	0·0524	0542	0559	0577	0594	0612	0629	0647	0664	0682	0699	86	2	4	5	7	9	11	12	14	16
4	0·0699	0717	0734	0752	0769	0787	0805	0822	0840	0857	0875	85	2	4	5	7	9	11	12	14	16
5	0·0875	0892	0910	0928	0945	0963	0981	0998	1016	1033	1051	84	2	4	5	7	9	11	12	14	16
6	0·1051	1069	1086	1104	1122	1139	1157	1175	1192	1210	1228	83	2	4	5	7	9	11	12	14	16
7	0·1228	1246	1263	1281	1299	1317	1334	1352	1370	1388	1405	82	2	4	5	7	9	11	12	14	16
8	0·1405	1423	1441	1459	1477	1495	1512	1530	1548	1566	1584	81	2	4	5	7	9	11	12	14	16
9	0·1584	1602	1620	1638	1655	1673	1691	1709	1727	1745	1763	80	2	4	5	7	9	11	13	14	16
10	0·1763	1781	1799	1817	1835	1853	1871	1890	1908	1926	1944	79	2	4	5	7	9	11	13	14	16
11	0·1944	1962	1980	1998	2016	2035	2053	2071	2089	2107	2126	78	2	4	5	7	9	11	13	15	16
12	0·2126	2144	2162	2180	2199	2217	2235	2254	2272	2290	2309	77	2	4	5	7	9	11	13	15	16
13	0·2309	2327	2345	2364	2382	2401	2419	2438	2456	2475	2493	76	2	4	6	7	9	11	13	15	17
14	0·2493	2512	2530	2549	2568	2586	2605	2623	2642	2661	2679	75	2	4	6	7	9	11	13	15	17
15	0·2679	2698	2717	2736	2754	2773	2792	2811	2830	2849	2867	74	2	4	6	8	9	11	13	15	17
16	0·2867	2886	2905	2924	2943	2962	2981	3000	3019	3038	3057	73	2	4	6	8	9	11	13	15	17
17	0·3057	3076	3096	3115	3134	3153	3172	3191	3211	3230	3249	72	2	4	6	8	10	12	13	15	
18	0·3249	3269	3288	3307	3327	3346	3365	3385	3404	3424	3443	71	2	4	6	8	10	12	14	16	
19	0·3443	3463	3482	3502	3522	3541	3561	3581	3600	3620	3640	70	2	4	6	8	10	12	14	16	
20	0·3640	3659	3679	3699	3719	3739	3759	3779	3799	3819	3839	69	2	4	6	8	10	12	14	16	
21	0·3839	3859	3879	3899	3919	3939	3959	3979	4000	4020	4040	68	2	4	6	8	10	12	14	16	
22	0·4040	4061	4081	4101	4122	4142	4163	4183	4204	4224	4245	67	2	4	6	8	10	12	14	16	
23	0·4245	4265	4286	4307	4327	4348	4369	4390	4411	4431	4452	66	2	4	6	8	10	12	15	17	
24	0·4452	4473	4494	4515	4536	4557	4578	4599	4621	4642	4663	65	2	4	6	8	11	13	15	17	
25	0·4663	4684	4706	4727	4748	4770	4791	4813	4834	4856	4877	64	2	4	6	9	11	13	15	17	
26	0·4877	4899	4921	4942	4964	4986	5008	5029	5051	5073	5095	63	2	4	7	9	11	13	15		
27	0·5095	5117	5139	5161	5184	5206	5228	5250	5272	5295	5317	62	2	4	7	9	11	13	16	18	
28	0·5317	5340	5362	5384	5407	5430	5452	5475	5498	5520	5543	61	2	5	7	9	11	14	16	18	
29	0·5543	5566	5589	5612	5635	5658	5681	5704	5727	5750	5774	60	2	5	7	9	12	14	16	18	
30	0·5774	5797	5820	5844	5867	5890	5914	5938	5961	5985	6009	59	2	5	7	9	12	14	16	19	
31	0·6009	6032	6056	6080	6104	6128	6152	6176	6200	6224	6249	58	2	5	7	10	12	14	17	19	
32	0·6249	6273	6297	6322	6346	6371	6395	6420	6445	6469	6494	57	2	5	7	10	12	15	17	20	
33	0·6494	6519	6544	6569	6594	6619	6644	6669	6694	6720	6745	56	3	5	8	10	13	15	18	20	
34	0·6745	6771	6796	6822	6847	6873	6899	6924	6950	6976	7002	55	3	5	8	10	13	15	18	21	
35	0·7002	7028	7054	7080	7107	7133	7159	7186	7212	7239	7265	54	3	5	8	11	13	16	18	21	
36	0·7265	7292	7319	7346	7373	7400	7427	7454	7481	7508	7536	53	3	5	8	11	14	16	19	22	
37	0·7536	7563	7590	7618	7646	7673	7701	7729	7757	7785	7813	52	3	6	8	11	14	17	19	22	
38	0·7813	7841	7869	7898	7926	7954	7983	8012	8040	8069	8098	51	3	6	9	11	14	17	20	23	
39	0·8098	8127	8156	8185	8214	8243	8273	8302	8332	8361	8391	50	3	6	9	12	15	18	21	23	
40	0·8391	8421	8451	8481	8511	8541	8571	8601	8632	8662	8693	49	3	6	9	12	15	18	21	24	
41	0·8693	8724	8754	8785	8816	8847	8878	8910	8941	8972	9004	48	3	6	9	12	16	19	22	25	
42	0·9004	9036	9067	9099	9131	9163	9195	9228	9260	9293	9325	47	3	6	10	13	16	19	22	26	
43	0·9325	9358	9391	9424	9457	9490	9523	9556	9590	9623	9657	46	3	7	10	13	17	20	23	27	
	1·0	·9	·8	·7	·6	·5	·4	·3	·2	·1	·0		1	2	3	4	5	6	7	8	

NATURAL COTANGENTS

NATURAL TANGENTS

	·0	·1	·2	·3	·4	·5	·6	·7	·8	·9	1·0		1	2	3	4	5	6	7	8	9
44°	0·9657	9691	9725	9759	9793	9827	9861	9896	9930	9965	0000	45°	3	7	10	14	17	21	24	27	31
45	1·0000	0035	0070	0105	0141	0176	0212	0247	0283	0319	0355	44	4	7	11	14	18	21	25	28	32
46	1·0355	0392	0428	0464	0501	0538	0575	0612	0649	0686	0724	43	4	7	11	15	18	22	26	29	33
47	1·0724	0761	0799	0837	0875	0913	0951	0990	1028	1067	1106	42	4	8	11	15	19	23	27	31	34
48	1·1106	1145	1184	1224	1263	1303	1343	1383	1423	1463	1504	41	4	8	12	16	20	24	28	32	36
49	1·1504	1544	1585	1626	1667	1708	1750	1792	1833	1875	1918	40	4	8	12	17	21	25	29	33	37
50	1·1918	1960	2002	2045	2088	2131	2174	2218	2261	2305	2349	39	4	9	13	17	22	26	30	35	39
51	1·2349	2393	2437	2482	2527	2572	2617	2662	2708	2753	2799	38	5	9	14	18	23	27	32	36	41
52	1·2799	2846	2892	2938	2985	3032	3079	3127	3175	3222	3270	37	5	9	14	19	24	28	33	38	42
53	1·3270	3319	3367	3416	3465	3514	3564	3613	3663	3713	3764	36	5	10	15	20	25	30	35	39	44
54	1·3764	3814	3865	3916	3968	4019	4071	4124	4176	4229	4281	35	5	10	16	21	26	31	36	41	47
55	1·4281	4335	4388	4442	4496	4550	4605	4659	4715	4770	4826	34	5	11	16	22	27	33	38	44	49
56	1·4826	4882	4938	4994	5051	5108	5166	5224	5282	5340	5399	33	6	11	17	23	29	34	40	46	52
57	1·5399	5458	5517	5577	5637	5697	5757	5818	5880	5941	6003	32	6	12	18	24	30	36	42	48	54
58	1·6003	6066	6128	6191	6255	6319	6383	6447	6512	6577	6643	31	6	13	19	26	32	38	45	51	58
59	1·6643	6709	6775	6842	6909	6977	7045	7113	7182	7251	7321	30	7	14	20	27	34	41	47	54	61
60	1·7321	7391	7461	7532	7603	7675	7747	7820	7893	7966	8040	29	7	14	22	29	36	43	50	58	65
61	1·8040	8115	8190	8265	8341	8418	8495	8572	8650	8728	8807	28	8	15	23	31	38	46	54	61	69
62	1·8807	8887	8967	9047	9128	9210	9292	9375	9458	9542	9626	27	8	16	25	33	41	49	57	66	74
63	1·9626	9711	9797	9883	9970	0057	0145	0233	0323	0413	0503	26	9	18	26	35	44	53	61	70	79
64	2·0503	0594	0686	0778	0872	0965	1060	1155	1251	1348	1445	25	9	19	28	38	47	57	66	75	85
65	2·1445	1543	1642	1742	1842	1943	2045	2148	2251	2355	2460	24	10	20	30	41	51	61	71	81	91
66	2·2460	2566	2673	2781	2889	2998	3109	3220	3332	3445	3559	23	11	22	33	44	55	66	77	88	99
67	2·3559	3673	3789	3906	4023	4142	4262	4383	4504	4627	4751	22									
68	2·4751	4876	5002	5129	5257	5386	5517	5649	5782	5916	6051	21									
69	2·6051	6187	6325	6464	6605	6746	6889	7034	7179	7326	7475	20									
70	2·7475	7625	7776	7929	8083	8239	8397	8556	8716	8878	9042	19									
71	2·9042	9208	9375	9544	9714	9887	0061	0237	0415	0595	0777	18									
72	3·0777	0961	1146	1334	1524	1716	1910	2106	2305	2506	2709	17									
73	3·2709	2914	3122	3332	3544	3759	3977	4197	4420	4646	4874	16									
74	3·4874	5105	5339	5576	5816	6059	6305	6554	6806	7062	7321	15									
75	3·7321	7583	7848	8118	8391	8667	8947	9232	9520	9812	0108	14									
76	4·0108	0408	0713	1022	1335	1653	1976	2303	2635	2972	3315	13									
77	4·3315	3662	4015	4373	4737	5107	5483	5864	6252	6646	7046	12									
78	4·7046	7453	7867	8288	8716	9152	9594	0045	0504	0970	1446	11									
79	5·1446	1929	2422	2924	3435	3955	4486	5026	5578	6140	6713	10									
80	5·671	5·730	5·789	5·850	5·912	5·976	6·041	6·107	6·174	6·243	6·314	9									
81	6·314	6·386	6·460	6·535	6·612	6·691	6·772	6·855	6·940	7·026	7·115	8									
82	7·115	7·207	7·300	7·396	7·495	7·596	7·700	7·806	7·916	8·028	8·144	7									
83	8·144	8·264	8·386	8·513	8·643	8·777	8·915	9·058	9·205	9·357	9·514	6									
84	9·514	9·677	9·845	10·019	10·199	10·385	10·579	10·780	10·988	11·205	11·430	5									
85	11·430	11·664	11·909	12·163	12·429	12·706	12·996	13·300	13·617	13·951	14·301	4									
86	14·301	14·669	15·056	15·464	15·895	16·350	16·832	17·343	17·886	18·464	19·081	3									
87	19·081	19·740	20·446	21·205	22·022	22·904	23·859	24·898	26·031	27·271	28·636	2									
88	28·636	30·145	31·821	33·694	35·801	38·188	40·917	44·066	47·740	52·081	57·290	1									
89	57·29	63·66	71·62	81·85	95·49	114·59	143·24	190·98	286·48	572·96		0									
	1·0	·9	·8	·7	·6	·5	·4	·3	·2	·1	·0		1	2	3	4	5	6	7	8	9

Use
Linear
Interpolation

NATURAL COTANGENTS

NATURAL SECANTS

	·0	·1	·2	·3	·4	·5	·6	·7	·8	·9	1·0		1	2	3	4	5	6	7	8	9
0°	1·0000	0000	0000	0000	0000	0000	0001	0001	0001	0001	0002	89°	0	0	0	0	0	0	0	0	0
1	1·0002	0002	0002	0003	0003	0003	0004	0004	0005	0006	0006	88	0	0	0	0	0	0	0	0	0
2	1·0006	0007	0007	0008	0009	0010	0010	0011	0012	0013	0014	87	0	0	0	0	0	0	1	1	1
3	1·0014	0015	0016	0017	0018	0019	0020	0021	0022	0023	0024	86	0	0	0	0	1	1	1	1	1
4	1·0024	0026	0027	0028	0030	0031	0032	0034	0035	0037	0038	85	0	0	0	1	1	1	1	1	1
5	1·0038	0040	0041	0043	0045	0046	0048	0050	0051	0053	0055	84	0	0	1	1	1	1	1	1	2
6	1·0055	0057	0059	0061	0063	0065	0067	0069	0071	0073	0075	83	0	0	1	1	1	1	1	2	2
7	1·0075	0077	0079	0082	0084	0086	0089	0091	0093	0096	0098	82	0	0	1	1	1	1	2	2	2
8	1·0098	0101	0103	0106	0108	0111	0114	0116	0119	0122	0125	81	0	1	1	1	1	2	2	2	2
9	1·0125	0127	0130	0133	0136	0139	0142	0145	0148	0151	0154	80	0	1	1	1	1	2	2	2	3
10	1·0154	0157	0161	0164	0167	0170	0174	0177	0180	0184	0187	79	0	1	1	1	2	2	2	3	3
11	1·0187	0191	0194	0198	0201	0205	0209	0212	0216	0220	0223	78	0	1	1	1	2	2	3	3	3
12	1·0223	0227	0231	0235	0239	0243	0247	0251	0255	0259	0263	77	0	1	1	2	2	2	3	3	4
13	1·0263	0267	0271	0276	0280	0284	0288	0293	0297	0302	0306	76	0	1	1	2	2	3	3	3	4
14	1·0306	0311	0315	0320	0324	0329	0334	0338	0343	0348	0353	75	0	1	1	2	2	3	3	4	4
15	1·0353	0358	0363	0367	0372	0377	0382	0388	0393	0398	0403	74	1	1	2	2	3	3	4	4	5
16	1·0403	0408	0413	0419	0424	0429	0435	0440	0446	0451	0457	73	1	1	2	2	3	3	4	4	5
17	1·0457	0463	0468	0474	0480	0485	0491	0497	0503	0509	0515	72	1	1	2	2	3	3	4	5	5
18	1·0515	0521	0527	0533	0539	0545	0551	0557	0564	0570	0576	71	1	1	2	2	3	4	4	5	6
19	1·0576	0583	0589	0595	0602	0608	0615	0622	0628	0635	0642	70	1	1	2	3	3	4	5	5	6
20	1·0642	0649	0655	0662	0669	0676	0683	0690	0697	0704	0711	69	1	1	2	3	3	4	5	6	6
21	1·0711	0719	0726	0733	0740	0748	0755	0763	0770	0778	0785	68	1	1	2	3	4	4	5	6	7
22	1·0785	0793	0801	0808	0816	0824	0832	0840	0848	0856	0864	67	1	2	2	3	4	5	5	6	7
23	1·0864	0872	0880	0888	0896	0904	0913	0921	0929	0938	0946	66	1	2	2	3	4	5	6	7	7
24	1·0946	0955	0963	0972	0981	0989	0998	1007	1016	1025	1034	65	1	2	3	3	4	5	6	7	8
25	1·1034	1043	1052	1061	1070	1079	1089	1098	1107	1117	1126	64	1	2	3	4	5	6	6	7	8
26	1·1126	1136	1145	1155	1164	1174	1184	1194	1203	1213	1223	63	1	2	3	4	5	6	7	8	9
27	1·1223	1233	1243	1253	1264	1274	1284	1294	1305	1315	1326	62	1	2	3	4	5	6	7	8	9
28	1·1326	1336	1347	1357	1368	1379	1390	1401	1412	1423	1434	61	1	2	3	4	5	6	8	9	10
29	1·1434	1445	1456	1467	1478	1490	1501	1512	1524	1535	1547	60	1	2	3	5	6	7	8	9	10
30	1·1547	1559	1570	1582	1594	1606	1618	1630	1642	1654	1666	59	1	2	4	5	6	7	8	10	11
31	1·1666	1679	1691	1703	1716	1728	1741	1753	1766	1779	1792	58	1	3	4	5	6	8	9	10	11
32	1·1792	1805	1818	1831	1844	1857	1870	1883	1897	1910	1924	57	1	3	4	5	7	8	9	11	12
33	1·1924	1937	1951	1964	1978	1992	2006	2020	2034	2048	2062	56	1	3	4	6	7	8	10	11	12
34	1·2062	2076	2091	2105	2120	2134	2149	2163	2178	2193	2208	55	1	3	4	6	7	9	10	12	13
35	1·2208	2223	2238	2253	2268	2283	2299	2314	2329	2345	2361	54	2	3	5	6	8	9	11	12	14
36	1·2361	2376	2392	2408	2424	2440	2456	2472	2489	2505	2521	53	2	3	5	6	8	10	11	13	14
37	1·2521	2538	2554	2571	2588	2605	2622	2639	2656	2673	2690	52	2	3	5	7	8	10	12	14	15
38	1·2690	2708	2725	2742	2760	2778	2796	2813	2831	2849	2868	51	2	4	5	7	9	11	12	14	16
39	1·2868	2886	2904	2923	2941	2960	2978	2997	3016	3035	3054	50	2	4	6	7	9	11	13	15	17
40	1·3054	3073	3093	3112	3131	3151	3171	3190	3210	3230	3250	49	2	4	6	8	10	12	14	16	18
41	1·3250	3270	3291	3311	3331	3352	3373	3393	3414	3435	3456	48	2	4	6	8	10	12	14	16	18
42	1·3456	3478	3499	3520	3542	3563	3585	3607	3629	3651	3673	47	2	4	7	9	11	13	15	17	20
43	1·3673	3696	3718	3741	3763	3786	3809	3832	3855	3878	3902	46	2	5	7	9	11	14	16	18	20
	1·0	·9	·8	·7	·6	·5	·4	·3	·2	·1	·0		1	2	3	4	5	6	7	8	9

NATURAL COSECANTS

	·0	·1	·2	·3	·4	·5	·6	·7	·8	·9	1·0		1	2	3	4	5	6	7	8	9
44°	1·3902	3925	3949	3972	3996	4020	4044	4069	4093	4118	4142	45°	2	5	7	10	12	14	17	19	22
45	1·4142	4167	4192	4217	4242	4267	4293	4318	4344	4370	4396	44	3	5	8	10	13	15	18	20	23
46	1·4396	4422	4448	4474	4501	4527	4554	4581	4608	4635	4663	43	3	5	8	11	13	16	19	21	24
47	1·4663	4690	4718	4746	4774	4802	4830	4859	4887	4916	4945	42	3	6	8	11	14	17	20	23	25
48	1·4945	4974	5003	5032	5062	5092	5121	5151	5182	5212	5243	41	3	6	9	12	15	18	21	24	27
49	1·5243	5273	5304	5335	5366	5398	5429	5461	5493	5525	5557	40	3	6	9	13	16	19	22	25	28
50	1·5557	5590	5622	5655	5688	5721	5755	5788	5822	5856	5890	39	3	7	10	13	17	20	23	27	30
51	1·5890	5925	5959	5994	6029	6064	6099	6135	6171	6207	6243	38	4	7	11	14	18	21	25	28	32
52	1·6243	6279	6316	6353	6390	6427	6464	6502	6540	6578	6616	37	4	7	11	15	19	22	26	30	34
53	1·6616	6655	6694	6733	6772	6812	6852	6892	6932	6972	7013	36	4	8	12	16	20	24	28	32	36
54	1·7013	7054	7095	7137	7179	7221	7263	7305	7348	7391	7434	35	4	8	13	17	21	25	30	34	38
55	1·7434	7478	7522	7566	7610	7655	7700	7745	7791	7837	7883	34	4	9	13	18	22	27	31	36	40
56	1·7883	7929	7976	8023	8070	8118	8166	8214	8263	8312	8361	33	5	10	14	19	24	29	33	38	43
57	1·8361	8410	8460	8510	8561	8612	8663	8714	8766	8818	8871	32	5	10	15	20	26	31	36	41	46
58	1·8871	8924	8977	9031	9084	9139	9194	9249	9304	9360	9416	31	5	11	16	22	27	33	38	44	49
59	1·9416	9473	9530	9587	9645	9703	9762	9821	9880	9940	0000	30	6	12	18	23	29	35	41	47	53
60	2·0000	0061	0122	0183	0245	0308	0371	0434	0498	0562	0627	29	6	13	19	25	31	38	44	50	56
61	2·0627	0692	0757	0824	0890	0957	1025	1093	1162	1231	1301	28	7	13	20	27	34	40	47	54	61
62	2·1301	1371	1441	1513	1584	1657	1730	1803	1877	1952	2027	27	7	15	22	29	36	44	51	58	65
63	2·2027	2103	2179	2256	2333	2412	2490	2570	2650	2730	2812	26	8	16	24	31	39	47	55	63	71
64	2·2812	2894	2976	3060	3144	3228	3314	3400	3486	3574	3662	25	9	17	26	34	43	51	60	68	77
65	2·3662	3751	3841	3931	4022	4114	4207	4300	4395	4490	4586	24	9	18	28	37	46	55	65	74	83
66	2·4586	4683	4780	4879	4978	5078	5180	5282	5384	5488	5593	23	10	20	30	40	50	60	70	81	91
67	2·5593	5699	5805	5913	6022	6131	6242	6354	6466	6580	6695	22									
68	2·6695	6811	6927	7046	7165	7285	7407	7529	7653	7778	7904	21									
69	2·7904	8032	8161	8291	8422	8555	8688	8824	8960	9099	9238	20									
70	2·9238	9379	9521	9665	9811	9957	0106	0256	0407	0561	0716	19									
71	3·0716	0872	1030	1190	1352	1515	1681	1848	2017	2188	2361	18									
72	3·2361	2535	2712	2891	3072	3255	3440	3628	3817	4009	4203	17									
73	3·4203	4399	4598	4799	5003	5209	5418	5629	5843	6060	6280	16									
74	3·6280	6502	6727	6955	7186	7420	7657	7897	8140	8387	8637	15									
75	3·8637	8890	9147	9408	9672	9939	0211	0486	0765	1048	1336	14									
76	4·1336	1627	1923	2223	2527	2837	3150	3469	3792	4121	4454	13									
77	4·4454	4793	5137	5486	5841	6202	6569	6942	7321	7706	8097	12									
78	4·8097	8496	8901	9313	9732	0159	0593	1034	1484	1942	2408	11									
79	5·2408	2883	3367	3860	4362	4874	5396	5928	6470	7023	7588	10									
80	5·759	5·816	5·875	5·935	5·996	6·059	6·123	6·188	6·255	6·323	6·392	9									
81	6·392	6·464	6·537	6·611	6·687	6·765	6·845	6·927	7·011	7·097	7·185	8									
82	7·185	7·276	7·368	7·463	7·561	7·661	7·764	7·870	7·979	8·091	8·206	7									
83	8·206	8·324	8·446	8·571	8·700	8·834	8·971	9·113	9·259	9·411	9·567	6									
84	9·567	9·728	9·895	10·068	10·248	10·433	10·626	10·826	11·034	11·249	11·474	5									
85	11·474	11·707	11·951	12·204	12·469	12·745	13·035	13·337	13·654	13·987	14·336	4									
86	14·336	14·703	15·089	15·496	15·926	16·380	16·862	17·372	17·914	18·492	19·107	3									
87	19·107	19·766	20·471	21·229	22·044	22·926	23·880	24·918	26·050	27·290	28·654	2									
88	28·654	30·161	31·836	33·708	35·815	38·202	40·930	44·077	47·750	52·090	57·299	1									
89	57·30	63·66	71·62	81·85	95·49	114·59	143·24	190·99	286·48	572·96		0									
	1·0	·9	·8	·7	·6	·5	·4	·3	·2	·1	·0		1	2	3	4	5	6	7	8	9

Use
Linear
Interpolation

NATURAL COSECANTS

DEGREES TO RADIANS

Degrees	Radians	Degrees	Radians	Degrees	Radians	Degrees	Radians
0	0·0000	23	0·4014	46	0·8029	69	1·2043
1	0·0175	24	0·4189	47	0·8203	70	1·2217
2	0·0349	25	0·4363	48	0·8378	71	1·2392
3	0·0524	26	0·4538	49	0·8552	72	1·2566
4	0·0698	27	0·4712	50	0·8727	73	1·2741
5	0·0873	28	0·4887	51	0·8901	74	1·2915
6	0·1047	29	0·5061	52	0·9076	75	1·3090
7	0·1222	30	0·5236	53	0·9250	76	1·3265
8	0·1396	31	0·5411	54	0·9425	77	1·3439
9	0·1571	32	0·5585	55	0·9599	78	1·3614
10	0·1745	33	0·5760	56	0·9774	79	1·3788
11	0·1920	34	0·5934	57	0·9948	80	1·3963
12	0·2094	35	0·6109	58	1·0123	81	1·4137
13	0·2269	36	0·6283	59	1·0297	82	1·4312
14	0·2443	37	0·6458	60	1·0472	83	1·4486
15	0·2618	38	0·6632	61	1·0647	84	1·4661
16	0·2793	39	0·6807	62	1·0821	85	1·4835
17	0·2967	40	0·6981	63	1·0996	86	1·5010
18	0·3142	41	0·7156	64	1·1170	87	1·5184
19	0·3316	42	0·7330	65	1·1345	88	1·5359
20	0·3491	43	0·7505	66	1·1519	89	1·5533
21	0·3665	44	0·7679	67	1·1694	90	1·5708
22	0·3840	45	0·7854	68	1·1868		

MINUTES TO RADIANS

Minutes	Radians	Minutes	Radians	Minutes	Radians
1	0·0003	6	0·0017	20	0·0058
2	0·0006	7	0·0020	30	0·0087
3	0·0009	8	0·0023	40	0·0116
4	0·0012	9	0·0026	50	0·0145
5	0·0015	10	0·0029	60	0·0175

To convert degrees and minutes to radians for angles other than those given in these tables, use linear interpolation.

RADIANS TO DEGREES

Radians	Degrees	Radians	Degrees	Radians	Degrees	Radians	Degrees
0·0	0·0000	0·8	45·8366	1·6	91·6732	2·4	137·5099
0·1	5·7296	0·9	51·5662	1·7	97·4028	2·5	143·2394
0·2	11·4592	1·0	57·2958	1·8	103·1324	2·6	148·9690
0·3	17·1887	1·1	63·0254	1·9	108·8620	2·7	154·6986
0·4	22·9183	1·2	68·7549	2·0	114·5916	2·8	160·4282
0·5	28·6479	1·3	74·4845	2·1	120·3211	2·9	166·1578
0·6	34·3775	1·4	80·2141	2·2	126·0507	3·0	171·8873
0·7	40·1070	1·5	85·9437	2·3	131·7803	3·1	177·6169
						3·2	183·3465

To convert radians to degrees for angles other than those given in this table, use linear interpolation.

TABLES OF CIRCULAR AND EXPONENTIAL FUNCTIONS

A NOTE ON INTERPOLATION

To save space, no mean differences are given for these tables (pp. 30 and 32). Values for the functions at intermediate points of the domain may be found by using the local first-order approximation

$$f(p+\alpha) \approx f(p)+f'(p) \times \alpha,$$

which is particularly simple for these functions since the values of $f'(p)$ are available in the same set of tables as those of $f(p)$. The resulting formulae are:

(1) $\sin(p+\alpha) \approx \sin p + \cos p \times \alpha$;

(2) $\cos(p+\alpha) \approx \cos p + (-\sin p) \times \alpha$;

(3) $e^{p+\alpha} \approx e^p + e^p \times \alpha$;

(4) $e^{-(p+\alpha)} \approx e^{-p} + (-e^{-p}) \times \alpha$;

(5) $\sinh(p+\alpha) \approx \sinh p + \cosh p \times \alpha$;

(6) $\cosh(p+\alpha) \approx \cosh p + \sinh p \times \alpha$.

The method is illustrated by the following examples.

(i) *To evaluate sin 0·853.* Use formula (1) with $p = 0.85$ and $\alpha = 0.003$. From the tables $\sin 0.85 = 0.7513$ and $\cos 0.85 = 0.6600$, so that

$$\sin 0.853 \approx 0.7513 + 0.6600 \times 0.003$$

$$\approx 0.7513 + 0.0020 = \mathbf{0.7533}.$$

(ii) *To evaluate cos 0·328.* Write $0.328 = 0.33 + (-0.002)$, and use formula (2) with $p = 0.33$ and $\alpha = -0.002$. From the tables $\cos 0.33 = 0.9460$ and $\sin 0.33 = 0.3240$, so that

$$\cos 0.328 \approx 0.9460 + (-0.3240) \times (-0.002)$$

$$\approx 0.9460 + 0.0006 = \mathbf{0.9466}.$$

(iii) *To evaluate* $e^{-2.634}$. Use formula (4) with $p = 2.63$ and $\alpha = 0.004$. From the tables $e^{-2.63} = 0.07208$, so that

$$e^{-2.634} \approx 0.07208 + (-0.07208) \times 0.004$$

$$\approx 0.07208 - 0.00029 = \mathbf{0.07179}.$$

When this method of interpolation is applied to these particular functions, the method error (as distinct from the rounding error which is inseparable from the use of differencing methods in any form) is about $\frac{1}{2}\alpha^2$ times the tabulated value of the function itself. Since the value of $|\alpha|$ need never exceed 0·005, the greatest possible error is about 1.25×10^{-5} times $f(p)$, which is negligible with tables calculated to four significant figures. The method can therefore be used with confidence throughout the tabulated part of the domain.

Further explanation of the method will be found in *S.M.P. Advanced Mathematics*, reference 'local approximation'.

CIRCULAR FUNCTIONS

x	sin x	cos x	tan x	x	sin x	cos x	tan x
0·00	0·0000	1·0000	0·0000	0·55	0·5227	0·8525	0·6131
0·01	0·0100	1·0000	0·0100	0·56	0·5312	0·8473	0·6269
0·02	0·0200	0·9998	0·0200	0·57	0·5396	0·8419	0·6410
0·03	0·0300	0·9996	0·0300	0·58	0·5480	0·8365	0·6552
0·04	0·0400	0·9992	0·0400	0·59	0·5564	0·8309	0·6696
0·05	0·0500	0·9988	0·0500	0·60	0·5646	0·8253	0·6841
0·06	0·0600	0·9982	0·0601	0·61	0·5729	0·8196	0·6989
0·07	0·0699	0·9976	0·0701	0·62	0·5810	0·8139	0·7139
0·08	0·0799	0·9968	0·0802	0·63	0·5891	0·8080	0·7291
0·09	0·0899	0·9960	0·0902	0·64	0·5972	0·8021	0·7445
0·10	0·0998	0·9950	0·1003	0·65	0·6052	0·7961	0·7602
0·11	0·1098	0·9940	0·1104	0·66	0·6131	0·7900	0·7761
0·12	0·1197	0·9928	0·1206	0·67	0·6210	0·7838	0·7923
0·13	0·1296	0·9916	0·1307	0·68	0·6288	0·7776	0·8087
0·14	0·1395	0·9902	0·1409	0·69	0·6365	0·7712	0·8253
0·15	0·1494	0·9888	0·1511	0·70	0·6442	0·7648	0·8423
0·16	0·1593	0·9872	0·1614	0·71	0·6518	0·7584	0·8595
0·17	0·1692	0·9856	0·1717	0·72	0·6594	0·7518	0·8771
0·18	0·1790	0·9838	0·1820	0·73	0·6669	0·7452	0·8949
0·19	0·1889	0·9820	0·1923	0·74	0·6743	0·7385	0·9131
0·20	0·1987	0·9801	0·2027	0·75	0·6816	0·7317	0·9316
0·21	0·2085	0·9780	0·2131	0·76	0·6889	0·7248	0·9505
0·22	0·2182	0·9759	0·2236	0·77	0·6961	0·7179	0·9697
0·23	0·2280	0·9737	0·2341	0·78	0·7033	0·7109	0·9893
0·24	0·2377	0·9713	0·2447	0·79	0·7104	0·7038	1·0092
0·25	0·2474	0·9689	0·2553	0·80	0·7174	0·6967	1·0296
0·26	0·2571	0·9664	0·2660	0·81	0·7243	0·6895	1·0505
0·27	0·2667	0·9638	0·2768	0·82	0·7311	0·6822	1·0717
0·28	0·2764	0·9611	0·2876	0·83	0·7379	0·6749	1·0934
0·29	0·2860	0·9582	0·2984	0·84	0·7446	0·6675	1·1156
0·30	0·2955	0·9553	0·3093	0·85	0·7513	0·6600	1·1383
0·31	0·3051	0·9523	0·3203	0·86	0·7578	0·6524	1·1616
0·32	0·3146	0·9492	0·3314	0·87	0·7643	0·6448	1·1853
0·33	0·3240	0·9460	0·3425	0·88	0·7707	0·6372	1·2097
0·34	0·3335	0·9428	0·3537	0·89	0·7771	0·6294	1·2346
0·35	0·3429	0·9394	0·3650	0·90	0·7833	0·6216	1·2602
0·36	0·3523	0·9359	0·3764	0·91	0·7895	0·6137	1·2864
0·37	0·3616	0·9323	0·3879	0·92	0·7956	0·6058	1·3133
0·38	0·3709	0·9287	0·3994	0·93	0·8016	0·5978	1·3409
0·39	0·3802	0·9249	0·4111	0·94	0·8076	0·5898	1·3692
0·40	0·3894	0·9211	0·4228	0·95	0·8134	0·5817	1·3984
0·41	0·3986	0·9171	0·4346	0·96	0·8192	0·5735	1·4284
0·42	0·4078	0·9131	0·4466	0·97	0·8249	0·5653	1·4592
0·43	0·4169	0·9090	0·4586	0·98	0·8305	0·5570	1·4910
0·44	0·4259	0·9048	0·4708	0·99	0·8360	0·5487	1·5237
0·45	0·4350	0·9004	0·4831	1·00	0·8415	0·5403	1·5574
0·46	0·4439	0·8961	0·4954	1·01	0·8468	0·5319	1·5922
0·47	0·4529	0·8916	0·5080	1·02	0·8521	0·5234	1·6281
0·48	0·4618	0·8870	0·5206	1·03	0·8573	0·5148	1·6652
0·49	0·4706	0·8823	0·5334	1·04	0·8624	0·5062	1·7036
0·50	0·4794	0·8776	0·5463	1·05	0·8674	0·4976	1·7433
0·51	0·4882	0·8727	0·5594	1·06	0·8724	0·4889	1·7844
0·52	0·4969	0·8678	0·5726	1·07	0·8772	0·4801	1·8270
0·53	0·5055	0·8628	0·5859	1·08	0·8820	0·4713	1·8712
0·54	0·5141	0·8577	0·5994	1·09	0·8866	0·4625	1·9171

CIRCULAR FUNCTIONS

x	$\sin x$	$\cos x$	$\tan x$	x	$\sin x$	$\cos x$	$\tan x$
1·10	0·8912	0·4536	1·9648	1·35	0·9757	0·2190	4·4552
1·11	0·8957	0·4447	2·0143	1·36	0·9779	0·2092	4·6734
1·12	0·9001	0·4357	2·0660	1·37	0·9799	0·1994	4·9131
1·13	0·9044	0·4267	2·1198	1·38	0·9819	0·1896	5·1774
1·14	0·9086	0·4176	2·1759	1·39	0·9837	0·1798	5·4707
1·15	0·9128	0·4085	2·2345	1·40	0·9854	0·1700	5·798
1·16	0·9168	0·3993	2·2958	1·41	0·9871	0·1601	6·165
1·17	0·9208	0·3902	2·3600	1·42	0·9887	0·1502	6·581
1·18	0·9246	0·3809	2·4273	1·43	0·9901	0·1403	7·056
1·19	0·9284	0·3717	2·4979	1·44	0·9915	0·1304	7·602
1·20	0·9320	0·3624	2·5722	1·45	0·9927	0·1205	8·238
1·21	0·9356	0·3530	2·6503	1·46	0·9939	0·1106	8·989
1·22	0·9391	0·3436	2·7328	1·47	0·9949	0·1006	9·887
1·23	0·9425	0·3342	2·8198	1·48	0·9959	0·0907	10·983
1·24	0·9458	0·3248	2·9119	1·49	0·9967	0·0807	12·35
1·25	0·9490	0·3153	3·0096	1·50	0·9975	0·0707	14·101
1·26	0·9521	0·3058	3·1133	1·51	0·9982	0·0608	16·428
1·27	0·9551	0·2963	3·2236	1·52	0·9987	0·0508	19·669
1·28	0·9580	0·2867	3·3413	1·53	0·9992	0·0408	24·498
1·29	0·9608	0·2771	3·4672	1·54	0·9995	0·0308	32·461
1·30	0·9636	0·2675	3·6021	1·55	0·9998	0·0208	48·079
1·31	0·9662	0·2579	3·7471	1·56	0·9999	0·0108	92·621
1·32	0·9687	0·2482	3·9033	1·57	1·0000	0·0008	1256
1·33	0·9711	0·2385	4·0723				
1·34	0·9735	0·2288	4·2556				

x	$\sin x$	$\cos x$	$\tan x$
$\pi/2$	1	0	
π	0	−1	0
$3\pi/2$	−1	0	
2π	0	1	0

EXPONENTIAL FUNCTIONS

x	e^x	e^{-x}	sinh x	cosh x
0·00	1·000	1·0000	0·00000	1·000
0·01	1·010	0·9900	0·01000	1·000
0·02	1·020	0·9802	0·02000	1·000
0·03	1·030	0·9704	0·03000	1·000
0·04	1·041	0·9608	0·04001	1·001
0·05	1·051	0·9512	0·05002	1·001
0·06	1·062	0·9418	0·06004	1·002
0·07	1·073	0·9324	0·07006	1·002
0·08	1·083	0·9231	0·08009	1·003
0·09	1·094	0·9139	0·09012	1·004
0·10	1·105	0·9048	0·1002	1·005
0·11	1·116	0·8958	0·1102	1·006
0·12	1·127	0·8869	0·1203	1·007
0·13	1·139	0·8781	0·1304	1·008
0·14	1·150	0·8694	0·1405	1·010
0·15	1·162	0·8607	0·1506	1·011
0·16	1·174	0·8521	0·1607	1·013
0·17	1·185	0·8437	0·1708	1·014
0·18	1·197	0·8353	0·1810	1·016
0·19	1·209	0·8270	0·1911	1·018
0·20	1·221	0·8187	0·2013	1·020
0·21	1·234	0·8106	0·2115	1·022
0·22	1·246	0·8025	·2218	1·024
0·23	1·259	0·7945	0·2320	1·027
0·24	1·271	0·7866	0·2423	1·029
0·25	1·284	0·7788	0·2526	1·031
0·26	1·297	0·7711	0·2629	1·034
0·27	1·310	0·7634	0·2733	1·037
0·28	1·323	0·7558	0·2837	1·039
0·29	1·336	0·7483	0·2941	1·042
0·30	1·350	0·7408	0·3045	1·045
0·31	1·363	0·7334	0·3150	1·048
0·32	1·377	0·7261	0·3255	1·052
0·33	1·391	0·7189	0·3360	1·055
0·34	1·405	0·7118	0·3466	1·058
0·35	1·419	0·7047	0·3572	1·062
0·36	1·433	0·6977	0·3678	1·066
0·37	1·448	0·6907	0·3785	1·069
0·38	1·462	0·6839	0·3892	1·073
0·39	1·477	0·6771	0·4000	1·077
0·40	1·492	0·6703	0·4108	1·081
0·41	1·507	0·6637	0·4216	1·085
0·42	1·522	0·6570	0·4325	1·090
0·43	1·537	0·6505	0·4434	1·094
0·44	1·553	0·6440	0·4543	1·098
0·45	1·568	0·6376	0·4653	1·103
0·46	1·584	0·6313	0·4764	1·108
0·47	1·600	0·6250	0·4875	1·112
0·48	1·616	0·6188	0·4986	1·117
0·49	1·632	0·6126	0·5098	1·122

x	e^x	e^{-x}	$\sinh x$	$\cosh x$
0·50	1·649	0·6065	0·5211	1·128
0·51	1·665	0·6005	0·5324	1·133
0·52	1·682	0·5945	0·5438	1·138
0·53	1·699	0·5886	0·5552	1·144
0·54	1·716	0·5827	0·5666	1·149
0·55	1·733	0·5769	0·5782	1·155
0·56	1·751	0·5712	0·5897	1·161
0·57	1·768	0·5655	0·6014	1·167
0·58	1·786	0·5599	0·6131	1·173
0·59	1·804	0·5543	0·6248	1·179
0·60	1·822	0·5488	0·6367	1·185
0·61	1·840	0·5434	0·6485	1·192
0·62	1·859	0·5379	0·6605	1·198
0·63	1·878	0·5326	0·6725	1·205
0·64	1·896	0·5273	0·6846	1·212
0·65	1·916	0·5220	0·6967	1·219
0·66	1·935	0·5169	0·7090	1·226
0·67	1·954	0·5117	0·7213	1·233
0·68	1·974	0·5066	0·7336	1·240
0·69	1·994	0·5016	0·7461	1·248
0·70	2·014	0·4966	0·7586	1·255
0·71	2·034	0·4916	0·7712	1·263
0·72	2·054	0·4868	0·7838	1·271
0·73	2·075	0·4819	0·7966	1·278
0·74	2·096	0·4771	0·8094	1·287
0·75	2·117	0·4724	0·8223	1·295
0·76	2·138	0·4677	0·8353	1·303
0·77	2·160	0·4630	0·8484	1·311
0·78	2·181	0·4584	0·8615	1·320
0·79	2·203	0·4538	0·8748	1·329
0·80	2·226	0·4493	0·8881	1·337
0·81	2·248	0·4449	0·9015	1·346
0·82	2·270	0·4404	0·9150	1·355
0·83	2·293	0·4360	0·9286	1·365
0·84	2·316	0·4317	0·9423	1·374
0·85	2·340	0·4274	0·9561	1·384
0·86	2·363	0·4232	0·9700	1·393
0·87	2·387	0·4190	0·9840	1·403
0·88	2·411	0·4148	0·9981	1·413
0·89	2·435	0·4107	1·012	1·423
0·90	2·460	0·4066	1·027	1·433
0·91	2·484	0·4025	1·041	1·443
0·92	2·509	0·3985	1·055	1·454
0·93	2·535	0·3946	1·070	1·465
0·94	2·560	0·3906	1·085	1·475
0·95	2·586	0·3867	1·099	1·486
0·96	2·612	0·3829	1·114	1·497
0·97	2·638	0·3791	1·129	1·509
0·98	2·664	0·3753	1·145	1·520
0·99	2·691	0·3716	1·160	1·531

x	e^x	e^{-x}	sinh x	cosh x
1·00	2·718	0·3679	1·175	1·543
1·01	2·746	0·3642	1·191	1·555
1·02	2·773	0·3606	1·206	1·567
1·03	2·801	0·3570	1·222	1·579
1·04	2·829	0·3535	1·238	1·591
1·05	2·858	0·3499	1·254	1·604
1·06	2·886	0·3465	1·270	1·616
1·07	2·915	0·3430	1·286	1·629
1·08	2·945	0·3396	1·303	1·642
1·09	2·974	0·3362	1·319	1·655
1·10	3·004	0·3329	1·336	1·669
1·11	3·034	0·3296	1·352	1·682
1·12	3·065	0·3263	1·369	1·696
1·13	3·096	0·3230	1·386	1·709
1·14	3·127	0·3198	1·403	1·723
1·15	3·158	0·3166	1·421	1·737
1·16	3·190	0·3135	1·438	1·752
1·17	3·222	0·3104	1·456	1·766
1·18	3·254	0·3073	1·474	1·781
1·19	3·287	0·3042	1·491	1·796
1·20	3·320	0·3012	1·509	1·811
1·21	3·353	0·2982	1·528	1·826
1·22	3·387	0·2952	1·546	1·841
1·23	3·421	0·2923	1·564	1·857
1·24	3·456	0·2894	1·583	1·872
1·25	3·490	0·2865	1·602	1·888
1·26	3·525	0·2837	1·621	1·905
1·27	3·561	0·2808	1·640	1·921
1·28	3·597	0·2780	1·659	1·937
1·29	3·633	0·2753	1·679	1·954
1·30	3·669	0·2725	1·698	1·971
1·31	3·706	0·2698	1·718	1·988
1·32	3·743	0·2671	1·738	2·005
1·33	3·781	0·2645	1·758	2·023
1·34	3·819	0·2618	1·779	2·040
1·35	3·857	0·2592	1·799	2·058
1·36	3·896	0·2567	1·820	2·076
1·37	3·935	0·2541	1·841	2·095
1·38	3·975	0·2516	1·862	2·113
1·39	4·015	0·2491	1·883	2·132
1·40	4·055	0·2466	1·904	2·151
1·41	4·096	0·2441	1·926	2·170
1·42	4·137	0·2417	1·948	2·189
1·43	4·179	0·2393	1·970	2·209
1·44	4·221	0·2369	1·992	2·229
1·45	4·263	0·2346	2·014	2·249
1·46	4·306	0·2322	2·037	2·269
1·47	4·349	0·2299	2·060	2·290
1·48	4·393	0·2276	2·083	2·310
1·49	4·437	0·2254	2·106	2·331

x	e^x	e^{-x}	$\sinh x$	$\cosh x$
1·50	4·482	0·2231	2·129	2·352
1·51	4·527	0·2209	2·153	2·374
1·52	4·572	0·2187	2·177	2·395
1·53	4·618	0·2165	2·201	2·417
1·54	4·665	0·2144	2·225	2·439
1·55	4·711	0·2122	2·250	2·462
1·56	4·759	0·2101	2·274	2·484
1·57	4·807	0·2080	2·299	2·507
1·58	4·855	0·2060	2·324	2·530
1·59	4·904	0·2039	2·350	2·554
1·60	4·953	0·2019	2·376	2·577
1·61	5·003	0·1999	2·401	2·601
1·62	5·053	0·1979	2·428	2·625
1·63	5·104	0·1959	2·454	2·650
1·64	5·155	0·1940	2·481	2·675
1·65	5·207	0·1920	2·507	2·700
1·66	5·259	0·1901	2·535	2·725
1·67	5·312	0·1882	2·562	2·750
1·68	5·366	0·1864	2·590	2·776
1·69	5·419	0·1845	2·617	2·802
1·70	5·474	0·1827	2·646	2·828
1·71	5·529	0·1809	2·674	2·855
1·72	5·585	0·1791	2·703	2·882
1·73	5·641	0·1773	2·732	2·909
1·74	5·697	0·1755	2·761	2·936
1·75	5·755	0·1738	2·790	2·964
1·76	5·812	0·1720	2·820	2·992
1·77	5·871	0·1703	2·850	3·021
1·78	5·930	0·1686	2·881	3·049
1·79	5·989	0·1670	2·911	3·078
1·80	6·050	0·1653	2·942	3·107
1·81	6·110	0·1637	2·973	3·137
1·82	6·172	0·1620	3·005	3·167
1·83	6·234	0·1604	3·037	3·197
1·84	6·297	0·1588	3·069	3·228
1·85	6·360	0·1572	3·101	3·259
1·86	6·424	0·1557	3·134	3·290
1·87	6·488	0·1541	3·167	3·321
1·88	6·554	0·1526	3·200	3·353
1·89	6·619	0·1511	3·234	3·385
1·90	6·686	0·1496	3·268	3·418
1·91	6·753	0·1481	3·303	3·451
1·92	6·821	0·1466	3·337	3·484
1·93	6·890	0·1451	3·372	3·517
1·94	6·959	0·1437	3·408	3·551
1·95	7·029	0·1423	3·443	3·585
1·96	7·099	0·1409	3·479	3·620
1·97	7·171	0·1395	3·516	3·655
1·98	7·243	0·1381	3·552	3·690
1·99	7·316	0·1367	3·589	3·726

x	e^x	e^{-x}	sinh x	cosh x
2·00	7·389	0·1353	3·627	3·762
2·01	7·463	0·1340	3·665	3·799
2·02	7·538	0·1327	3·703	3·835
2·03	7·614	0·1313	3·741	3·873
2·04	7·691	0·1300	3·780	3·910
2·05	7·768	0·1287	3·820	3·948
2·06	7·846	0·1275	3·859	3·987
2·07	7·925	0·1262	3·899	4·026
2·08	8·004	0·1249	3·940	4·065
2·09	8·085	0·1237	3·981	4·104
2·10	8·166	0·1225	4·022	4·144
2·11	8·248	0·1212	4·064	4·185
2·12	8·331	0·1200	4·106	4·226
2·13	8·415	0·1188	4·148	4·267
2·14	8·499	0·1177	4·191	4·309
2·15	8·585	0·1165	4·234	4·351
2·16	8·671	0·1153	4·278	4·393
2·17	8·758	0·1142	4·322	4·436
2·18	8·846	0·1130	4·367	4·480
2·19	8·935	0·1119	4·412	4·524
2·20	9·025	0·1108	4·457	4·568
2·21	9·116	0·1097	4·503	4·613
2·22	9·207	0·1086	4·549	4·658
2·23	9·300	0·1075	4·596	4·704
2·24	9·393	0·1065	4·643	4·750
2·25	9·488	0·1054	4·691	4·797
2·26	9·583	0·1044	4·739	4·844
2·27	9·679	0·1033	4·788	4·891
2·28	9·777	0·1023	4·837	4·939
2·29	9·875	0·1013	4·887	4·988
2·30	9·974	0·1003	4·937	5·037
2·31	10·07	0·09926	4·988	5·087
2·32	10·18	0·09827	5·039	5·137
2·33	10·28	0·09730	5·090	5·188
2·34	10·38	0·09633	5·142	5·239
2·35	10·49	0·09537	5·195	5·290
2·36	10·59	0·09442	5·248	5·343
2·37	10·70	0·09348	5·302	5·395
2·38	10·80	0·09255	5·356	5·449
2·39	10·91	0·09163	5·411	5·503
2·40	11·02	0·09072	5·466	5·557
2·41	11·13	0·08982	5·522	5·612
2·42	11·25	0·08892	5·578	5·667
2·43	11·36	0·08804	5·635	5·723
2·44	11·47	0·08716	5·693	5·780
2·45	11·59	0·08629	5·751	5·837
2·46	11·70	0·08543	5·810	5·895
2·47	11·82	0·08458	5·869	5·954
2·48	11·94	0·08374	5·929	6·013
2·49	12·06	0·08291	5·989	6·072

x	e^x	e^{-x}	$\sinh x$	$\cosh x$
2·50	12·18	0·08208	6·050	6·132
2·51	12·30	0·08127	6·112	6·193
2·52	12·43	0·08046	6·174	6·255
2·53	12·55	0·07966	6·237	6·317
2·54	12·68	0·07887	6·300	6·379
2·55	12·81	0·07808	6·365	6·443
2·56	12·94	0·07730	6·429	6·507
2·57	13·07	0·07654	6·495	6·571
2·58	13·20	0·07577	6·561	6·636
2·59	13·33	0·07502	6·627	6·702
2·60	13·46	0·07427	6·695	6·769
2·61	13·60	0·07353	6·763	6·836
2·62	13·74	0·07280	6·831	6·904
2·63	13·87	0·07208	6·901	6·973
2·64	14·01	0·07136	6·971	7·042
2·65	14·15	0·07065	7·042	7·112
2·66	14·30	0·06995	7·113	7·183
2·67	14·44	0·06925	7·185	7·255
2·68	14·59	0·06856	7·258	7·327
2·69	14·73	0·06788	7·332	7·400
2·70	14·88	0·06721	7·406	7·473
2·71	15·03	0·06654	7·481	7·548
2·72	15·18	0·06587	7·557	7·623
2·73	15·33	0·06522	7·634	7·699
2·74	15·49	0·06457	7·711	7·776
2·75	15·64	0·06393	7·789	7·853
2·76	15·80	0·06329	7·868	7·932
2·77	15·96	0·06266	7·948	8·011
2·78	16·12	0·06204	8·028	8·091
2·79	16·28	0·06142	8·110	8·171
2·80	16·44	0·06081	8·192	8·253
2·81	16·61	0·06020	8·275	8·335
2·82	16·78	0·05961	8·359	8·418
2·83	16·95	0·05901	8·443	8·502
2·84	17·12	0·05843	8·529	8·587
2·85	17·29	0·05784	8·615	8·673
2·86	17·46	0·05727	8·702	8·759
2·87	17·64	0·05670	8·790	8·847
2·88	17·81	0·05613	8·879	8·935
2·89	17·99	0·05558	8·969	9·024
2·90	18·17	0·05502	9·060	9·115
2·91	18·36	0·05448	9·151	9·206
2·92	18·54	0·05393	9·244	9·298
2·93	18·73	0·05340	9·337	9·391
2·94	18·92	0·05287	9·431	9·484
2·95	19·11	0·05234	9·572	9·579
2·96	19·30	0·05182	9·623	9·675
2·97	19·49	0·05130	9·720	9·772
2·98	19·69	0·05079	9·819	9·869
2·99	19·89	0·05029	9·918	9·968

x	e^x	e^{-x}	sinh x	cosh x
3·00	20·09	0·04979	10·02	10·07
3·01	20·29	0·04929	10·12	10·17
3·02	20·49	0·04880	10·22	10·27
3·03	20·70	0·04832	10·32	10·37
3·04	20·91	0·04783	10·43	10·48
3·05	21·12	0·04736	10·53	10·58
3·06	21·33	0·04689	10·64	10·69
3·07	21·54	0·04642	10·75	10·79
3·08	21·76	0·04596	10·86	10·90
3·09	21·98	0·04550	10·97	11·01
3·10	22·20	0·04505	11·08	11·12
3·11	22·42	0·04460	11·19	11·23
3·12	22·65	0·04416	11·30	11·35
3·13	22·87	0·04372	11·42	11·46
3·14	23·10	0·04328	11·53	11·57
3·15	23·34	0·04285	11·65	11·69
3·16	23·57	0·04243	11·76	11·81
3·17	23·81	0·04200	11·88	11·92
3·18	24·05	0·04159	12·00	12·04
3·19	24·29	0·04117	12·12	12·16
3·20	24·53	0·04076	12·25	12·29
3·21	24·78	0·04036	12·37	12·41
3·22	25·03	0·03996	12·49	12·53
3·23	25·28	0·03956	12·62	12·66
3·24	25·53	0·03916	12·75	12·79
3·25	25·79	0·03877	12·88	12·91
3·26	26·05	0·03839	13·01	13·04
3·27	26·31	0·03801	13·14	13·17
3·28	26·58	0·03763	13·27	13·31
3·29	26·84	0·03725	13·40	13·44
3·30	27·11	0·03688	13·54	13·57
3·31	27·39	0·03652	13·67	13·71
3·32	27·66	0·03615	13·81	13·85
3·33	27·94	0·03579	13·95	13·99
3·34	28·22	0·03544	14·09	14·13
3·35	28·50	0·03508	14·23	14·27
3·36	28·79	0·03474	14·38	14·41
3·37	29·08	0·03439	14·52	14·56
3·38	29·37	0·03405	14·67	14·70
3·39	29·67	0·03371	14·82	14·85
3·40	29·96	0·03337	14·97	15·00
3·41	30·27	0·03304	15·12	15·15
3·42	30·57	0·03271	15·27	15·30
3·43	30·88	0·03239	15·42	15·45
3·44	31·19	0·03206	15·58	15·61
3·45	31·50	0·03175	15·73	15·77
3·46	31·82	0·03143	15·89	15·92
3·47	32·14	0·03112	16·05	16·08
3·48	32·46	0·03081	16·21	16·25
3·49	32·79	0·03050	16·38	16·41

x	e^x	e^{-x}	sinh x	cosh x
3·50	33·12	0·03020	16·54	16·57
3·51	33·45	0·02990	16·71	16·74
3·52	33·78	0·02960	16·88	16·91
3·53	34·12	0·02930	17·05	17·08
3·54	34·47	0·02901	17·22	17·25
3·55	34·81	0·02872	17·39	17·42
3·56	35·16	0·02844	17·57	17·60
3·57	35·52	0·02816	17·74	17·77
3·58	35·87	0·02788	17·92	17·95
3·59	36·23	0·02760	18·10	18·13
3·60	36·60	0·02732	18·29	18·31
3·61	36·97	0·02705	18·47	18·50
3·62	37·34	0·02678	18·66	18·68
3·63	37·71	0·02652	18·84	18·87
3·64	38·09	0·02625	19·03	19·06
3·65	38·47	0·02599	19·22	19·25
3·66	38·86	0·02573	19·42	19·44
3·67	39·25	0·02548	19·61	19·64
3·68	39·65	0·02522	19·81	19·84
3·69	40·04	0·02497	20·01	20·03
3·70	40·45	0·02472	20·21	20·24
3·71	40·85	0·02448	20·41	20·44
3·72	41·26	0·02423	20·62	20·64
3·73	41·68	0·02399	20·83	20·85
3·74	42·10	0·02375	21·04	21·06
3·75	42·52	0·02352	21·25	21·27
3·76	42·95	0·02328	21·46	21·49
3·77	43·38	0·02305	21·68	21·70
3·78	43·82	0·02282	21·90	21·92
3·79	44·26	0·02260	22·12	22·14
3·80	44·70	0·02237	22·34	22·36
3·81	45·15	0·02215	22·56	22·59
3·82	45·60	0·02193	22·79	22·81
3·83	46·06	0·02171	23·02	23·04
3·84	46·53	0·02149	23·25	23·27
3·85	46·99	0·02128	23·49	23·51
3·86	47·47	0·02107	23·72	23·74
3·87	47·94	0·02086	23·96	23·98
3·88	48·42	0·02065	24·20	24·22
3·89	48·91	0·02045	24·45	24·47
3·90	49·40	0·02024	24·69	24·71
3·91	49·90	0·02004	24·94	24·96
3·92	50·40	0·01984	25·19	25·21
3·93	50·91	0·01964	25·44	25·46
3·94	51·42	0·01945	25·70	25·72
3·95	51·94	0·01925	25·96	25·98
3·96	52·46	0·01906	26·22	26·24
3·97	52·98	0·01887	26·48	26·50
3·98	53·52	0·01869	26·75	26·77
3·99	54·05	0·01850	27·02	27·04
4·00	54·60	0·01832	27·29	27·31

$$\sinh^{-1}x$$

x	0	1	2	3	4	5	6	7	8	9	1	2	3	4	5	6	7	8	9
0·0	0·0000	0100	0200	0300	0400	0500	0600	0699	0799	0899	10	20	30	40	50	60	70	80	90
0·1	0·0998	1098	1197	1296	1395	1494	1593	1692	1790	1889	10	20	30	40	49	59	69	79	89
0·2	0·1987	2085	2183	2280	2378	2475	2572	2668	2765	2861	10	19	29	39	49	58	68	78	87
0·3	0·2957	3052	3148	3243	3338	3432	3526	3620	3714	3807	9	19	28	38	47	57	66	76	85
0·4	0·3900	3993	4085	4177	4269	4360	4452	4542	4633	4722	9	18	27	37	46	55	64	73	82
0·5	0·4812	4901	4990	5079	5167	5255	5342	5429	5516	5602	9	18	26	35	44	53	61	70	79
0·6	0·5688	5774	5859	5944	6028	6112	6196	6279	6362	6445	8	17	25	34	42	50	59	67	76
0·7	0·6527	6608	6690	6771	6851	6931	7011	7091	7170	7248	8	16	24	32	40	48	56	64	72
0·8	0·7327	7405	7482	7559	7636	7712	7788	7864	7939	8014	8	15	23	31	38	46	53	61	69
0·9	0·8089	8163	8237	8310	8383	8456	8528	8600	8672	8743	7	15	22	29	36	44	51	58	65
1·0	0·8814	8884	8954	9024	9094	9163	9232	9300	9368	9436	7	14	21	28	35	41	48	55	62
1·1	0·9503	9571	9637	9704	9770	9836	9901	9966	0031	0096	7	13	20	26	33	39	46	53	59
1·2	1·0160	0224	0287	0350	0413	0476	0538	0600	0662	0723	6	13	19	25	31	38	44	50	56
1·3	1·0785	0845	0906	0966	1026	1086	1145	1204	1263	1322	6	12	18	24	30	36	42	48	54
1·4	1·1380	1438	1496	1553	1610	1667	1724	1780	1836	1892	6	11	17	23	28	34	40	46	51
1·5	1·1948	2003	2058	2113	2167	2222	2276	2330	2383	2437	5	11	16	22	27	33	38	43	49
1·6	1·2490	2543	2595	2648	2700	2752	2804	2855	2906	2957	5	10	16	21	26	31	36	42	47
1·7	1·3008	3059	3109	3159	3209	3259	3308	3358	3407	3456	5	10	15	20	25	30	35	40	45
1·8	1·3504	3553	3601	3649	3697	3745	3792	3839	3886	3933	5	10	14	19	24	29	33	38	43
1·9	1·3980	4026	4073	4119	4165	4210	4256	4301	4347	4392	5	9	14	18	23	27	32	37	41
2·0	1·4436	4481	4525	4570	4614	4658	4702	4745	4789	4832	4	9	13	18	22	26	31	35	40
2·1	1·4875	4918	4960	5003	5045	5088	5130	5172	5214	5255	4	8	13	17	21	25	30	34	38
2·2	1·5297	5338	5379	5420	5461	5502	5542	5583	5623	5663	4	8	12	16	20	24	28	33	37
2·3	1·5703	5743	5782	5822	5861	5900	5939	5978	6017	6056	4	8	12	16	20	24	27	31	35
2·4	1·6094	6133	6171	6209	6247	6285	6323	6360	6398	6435	4	8	11	15	19	23	27	30	34
2·5	1·6472	6509	6546	6583	6620	6656	6693	6729	6765	6801	4	7	11	15	18	22	26	29	33
2·6	1·6837	6873	6909	6945	6980	7015	7051	7086	7121	7156	4	7	11	14	18	21	25	28	32
2·7	1·7191	7225	7260	7294	7329	7363	7397	7431	7465	7499	3	7	10	14	17	21	24	27	31
2·8	1·7532	7566	7599	7633	7666	7699	7732	7765	7798	7831	3	7	10	13	17	20	23	27	30
2·9	1·7863	7896	7928	7961	7993	8025	8057	8089	8121	8153	3	6	10	13	16	19	23	26	29
3·0	1·8184	8216	8248	8279	8310	8341	8373	8404	8434	8465	3	6	9	12	16	19	22	25	28
3·1	1·8496	8527	8557	8588	8618	8648	8679	8709	8739	8769	3	6	9	12	15	18	21	24	27
3·2	1·8799	8828	8858	8888	8917	8947	8976	9005	9035	9064	3	6	9	12	15	18	21	24	27
3·3	1·9093	9122	9151	9179	9208	9237	9265	9294	9322	9351	3	6	9	11	14	17	20	23	26
3·4	1·9379	9407	9435	9463	9491	9519	9547	9574	9602	9630	3	6	8	11	14	17	20	22	25
3·5	1·9657	9685	9712	9739	9767	9794	9821	9848	9875	9902	3	5	8	11	14	16	19	22	24
3·6	1·9928	9955	9982	0008	0035	0061	0088	0114	0140	0166	3	5	8	11	13	16	19	21	24
3·7	2·0193	0219	0245	0271	0296	0322	0348	0374	0399	0425	3	5	8	10	13	15	18	21	23
3·8	2·0450	0476	0501	0526	0552	0577	0602	0627	0652	0677	3	5	8	10	13	15	18	20	23
3·9	2·0702	0727	0751	0776	0801	0825	0850	0874	0899	0923	2	5	7	10	12	15	17	20	22
4·0	2·0947	0971	0996	1020	1044	1068	1092	1116	1139	1163	2	5	7	10	12	14	17	19	22
4·1	2·1187	1211	1234	1258	1281	1305	1328	1351	1375	1398	2	5	7	9	12	14	16	19	21
4·2	2·1421	1444	1467	1490	1513	1536	1559	1582	1605	1627	2	5	7	9	11	14	16	18	21
4·3	2·1650	1673	1695	1718	1740	1763	1785	1808	1830	1852	2	4	7	9	11	13	16	18	20
4·4	2·1874	1896	1918	1940	1962	1984	2006	2028	2050	2072	2	4	7	9	11	13	15	18	20
4·5	2·2093	2115	2137	2158	2180	2201	2223	2244	2266	2287	2	4	6	9	11	13	15	17	19
4·6	2·2308	2329	2351	2372	2393	2414	2435	2456	2477	2498	2	4	6	8	11	13	15	17	19
4·7	2·2518	2539	2560	2581	2601	2622	2643	2663	2684	2704	2	4	6	8	10	12	14	16	19
4·8	2·2724	2745	2765	2785	2806	2826	2846	2866	2886	2906	2	4	6	8	10	12	14	16	18
4·9	2·2926	2946	2966	2986	3006	3026	3046	3065	3085	3105	2	4	6	8	10	12	14	16	18

x	0	1	2	3	4	5	6	7	8	9	1	2	3	4	5	6	7	8	9
5·0	2·3124	3144	3164	3183	3203	3222	3241	3261	3280	3299	2	4	6	8	10	12	14	16	17
5·1	2·3319	3338	3357	3376	3395	3414	3433	3452	3471	3490	2	4	6	8	10	11	13	15	17
5·2	2·3509	3528	3547	3566	3585	3603	3622	3641	3659	3678	2	4	6	7	9	11	13	15	17
5·3	2·3696	3715	3733	3752	3770	3789	3807	3825	3844	3862	2	4	6	7	9	11	13	15	17
5·4	2·3880	3898	3916	3935	3953	3971	3989	4007	4025	4043	2	4	5	7	9	11	13	14	16
5·5	2·4061	4078	4096	4114	4132	4150	4167	4185	4203	4220	2	4	5	7	9	11	12	14	16
5·6	2·4238	4255	4273	4291	4308	4325	4343	4360	4378	4395	2	3	5	7	9	10	12	14	16
5·7	2·4412	4429	4447	4464	4481	4498	4515	4532	4550	4567	2	3	5	7	9	10	12	14	15
5·8	2·4584	4601	4617	4634	4651	4668	4685	4702	4719	4735	2	3	5	7	8	10	12	13	15
5·9	2·4752	4769	4785	4802	4819	4835	4852	4868	4885	4901	2	3	5	7	8	10	12	13	15
6·0	2·4918	4934	4951	4967	4983	5000	5016	5032	5048	5065	2	3	5	7	8	10	11	13	15
6·1	2·5081	5097	5113	5129	5145	5161	5177	5193	5209	5225	2	3	5	6	8	10	11	13	14
6·2	2·5241	5257	5273	5289	5305	5321	5336	5352	5368	5384	2	3	5	6	8	9	11	13	14
6·3	2·5399	5415	5431	5446	5462	5477	5493	5509	5524	5539	2	3	5	6	8	9	11	12	14
6·4	2·5555	5570	5586	5601	5616	5632	5647	5662	5678	5693	2	3	5	6	8	9	11	12	14
6·5	2·5708	5723	5739	5754	5769	5784	5799	5814	5829	5844	2	3	5	6	8	9	11	12	14
6·6	2·5859	5874	5889	5904	5919	5934	5949	5963	5978	5993	1	3	4	6	7	9	10	12	13
6·7	2·6008	6023	6037	6052	6067	6081	6096	6111	6125	6140	1	3	4	6	7	9	10	12	13
6·8	2·6154	6169	6183	6198	6212	6227	6241	6256	6270	6284	1	3	4	6	7	9	10	12	13
6·9	2·6299	6313	6327	6342	6356	6370	6384	6399	6413	6427	1	3	4	6	7	9	10	11	13
7·0	2·6441	6455	6469	6484	6498	6512	6526	6540	6554	6568	1	3	4	6	7	8	10	11	13
7·1	2·6582	6596	6610	6623	6637	6651	6665	6679	6693	6706	1	3	4	6	7	8	10	11	12
7·2	2·6720	6734	6748	6761	6775	6789	6802	6816	6830	6843	1	3	4	5	7	8	10	11	12
7·3	2·6857	6870	6884	6897	6911	6924	6938	6951	6965	6978	1	3	4	5	7	8	9	11	12
7·4	2·6922	7005	7018	7032	7045	7058	7072	7085	7098	7111	1	3	4	5	7	8	9	11	12
7·5	2·7125	7138	7151	7164	7177	7191	7204	7217	7230	7243	1	3	4	5	7	8	9	11	12
7·6	2·7256	7269	7282	7295	7308	7321	7334	7347	7360	7373	1	3	4	5	6	8	9	10	12
7·7	2·7386	7398	7411	7424	7437	7450	7463	7475	7488	7501	1	3	4	5	6	8	9	10	12
7·8	2·7514	7526	7539	7552	7564	7577	7590	7602	7615	7627	1	3	4	5	6	8	9	10	11
7·9	2·7640	7652	7665	7678	7690	7703	7715	7727	7740	7752	1	2	4	5	6	7	9	10	11
8·0	2·7765	7777	7789	7802	7814	7827	7839	7851	7863	7876	1	2	4	5	6	7	9	10	11
8·1	2·7888	7900	7912	7925	7937	7949	7961	7973	7986	7998	1	2	4	5	6	7	9	10	11
8·2	2·8010	8022	8034	8046	8058	8070	8082	8094	8106	8118	1	2	4	5	6	7	8	10	11
8·3	2·8130	8142	8154	8166	8178	8190	8202	8214	8225	8237	1	2	4	5	6	7	8	10	11
8·4	2·8249	8261	8273	8284	8296	8308	8320	8331	8343	8355	1	2	4	5	6	7	8	9	11
8·5	2·8367	8378	8390	8402	8413	8425	8436	8448	8460	8471	1	2	3	5	6	7	8	9	10
8·6	2·8483	8494	8506	8517	8529	8540	8552	8563	8575	8586	1	2	3	5	6	7	8	9	10
8·7	2·8598	8609	8620	8632	8643	8655	8666	8677	8689	8700	1	2	3	5	6	7	8	9	10
8·8	2·8711	8722	8734	8745	8756	8767	8779	8790	8801	8812	1	2	3	4	6	7	8	9	10
8·9	2·8823	8835	8846	8857	8868	8879	8890	8901	8912	8923	1	2	3	4	6	7	8	9	10
9·0	2·8934	8945	8957	8968	8979	8990	9000	9011	9022	9033	1	2	3	4	5	7	8	9	10
9·1	2·9044	9055	9066	9077	9088	9099	9110	9120	9131	9142	1	2	3	4	5	7	8	9	10
9·2	2·9153	9164	9175	9185	9196	9207	9218	9228	9239	9250	1	2	3	4	5	6	8	9	10
9·3	2·9260	9271	9282	9292	9303	9314	9324	9335	9346	9356	1	2	3	4	5	6	7	9	10
9·4	2·9367	9377	9388	9398	9409	9419	9430	9441	9451	9462	1	2	3	4	5	6	7	8	9
9·5	2·9472	9482	9493	9503	9514	9524	9535	9545	9555	9566	1	2	3	4	5	6	7	8	9
9·6	2·9576	9586	9597	9607	9617	9628	9638	9648	9659	9669	1	2	3	4	5	6	7	8	9
9·7	2·9679	9689	9700	9710	9720	9730	9741	9751	9761	9771	1	2	3	4	5	6	7	8	9
9·8	2·9781	9791	9802	9812	9822	9832	9842	9852	9862	9872	1	2	3	4	5	6	7	8	9
9·9	2·9882	9892	9902	9912	9922	9932	9942	9952	9962	9972	1	2	3	4	5	6	7	8	9
10·0	2·9982	9992	0002	0012	0022	0032	0042	0052	0062	0071	1	2	3	4	5	6	7	8	9

Note: For values of x outside this range, use $\sinh^{-1}x = \ln\{x + \sqrt{(x^2+1)}\}$.

x	0	1	2	3	4	5	6	7	8	9	1	2	3	4	5	6	7	8	9
1·0	0·0000	1413	1997	2443	2819	3149	3447	3720	3974	4211	47	94	140	187	234	281	328	374	421
1·1	0·4436	4648	4851	5045	5232	5411	5584	5751	5913	6071	18	36	55	73	91	109	127	145	164
1·2	0·6224	6372	6517	6659	6797	6931	7063	7192	7319	7443	14	27	41	54	68	81	95	108	122
1·3	0·7564	7684	7801	7916	8029	8140	8249	8357	8463	8567	11	22	33	45	56	67	78	89	100
1·4	0·8670	8771	8871	8970	9067	9163	9258	9351	9443	9534	10	19	29	38	48	58	67	77	86
1·5	0·9624	9713	9801	9888	9974	0059	0143	0226	0308	0389	8	17	25	34	42	51	59	68	76
1·6	1·0470	0549	0628	0706	0784	0860	0936	1011	1086	1159	8	15	23	31	38	46	54	61	69
1·7	1·1232	1305	1376	1448	1518	1588	1657	1726	1794	1862	7	14	21	28	35	42	49	56	63
1·8	1·1929	1996	2062	2127	2192	2257	2321	2384	2447	2510	6	13	19	26	32	39	45	52	58
1·9	1·2572	2634	2695	2756	2816	2876	2935	2995	3053	3112	6	12	18	24	30	36	42	48	54
2·0	1·3170	3227	3284	3341	3397	3454	3509	3565	3620	3674	6	11	17	22	28	34	39	45	50
2·1	1·3729	3783	3836	3890	3943	3995	4048	4100	4152	4203	5	11	16	21	26	32	37	42	47
2·2	1·4254	4305	4356	4406	4456	4506	4555	4604	4653	4702	5	10	15	20	25	30	35	40	45
2·3	1·4750	4799	4846	4894	4942	4989	5036	5082	5129	5175	5	9	14	19	24	28	33	38	42
2·4	1·5221	5267	5312	5357	5402	5447	5492	5536	5580	5624	4	9	13	18	22	27	31	36	40
2·5	1·5668	5712	5755	5798	5841	5884	5926	5969	6011	6053	4	9	13	17	21	26	30	34	38
2·6	1·6094	6136	6177	6219	6260	6300	6341	6382	6422	6462	4	8	12	16	20	25	29	33	37
2·7	1·6502	6542	6581	6621	6660	6699	6738	6777	6816	6854	4	8	12	16	20	23	27	31	35
2·8	1·6892	6931	6969	7006	7044	7082	7119	7156	7193	7230	4	8	11	15	19	23	26	30	34
2·9	1·7267	7304	7340	7377	7413	7449	7485	7521	7556	7592	4	7	11	14	18	22	25	29	32
3·0	1·7627	7663	7698	7733	7768	7803	7837	7872	7906	7940	3	7	10	14	17	21	24	28	31
3·1	1·7975	8009	8042	8076	8110	8143	8177	8210	8243	8276	3	7	10	13	17	20	23	27	30
3·2	1·8309	8342	8375	8408	8440	8472	8505	8537	8569	8601	3	6	10	13	16	19	23	26	29
3·3	1·8633	8665	8696	8728	8759	8790	8822	8853	8884	8915	3	6	9	13	16	19	22	25	28
3·4	1·8946	8976	9007	9037	9068	9098	9128	9159	9189	9219	3	6	9	12	15	18	21	24	27
3·5	1·9248	9278	9308	9338	9367	9396	9426	9455	9484	9513	3	6	9	12	15	18	21	24	26
3·6	1·9542	9571	9600	9628	9657	9686	9714	9742	9771	9799	3	6	9	11	14	17	20	23	26
3·7	1·9827	9855	9883	9911	9939	9966	9994	0021	0049	0076	3	6	8	11	14	17	19	22	25
3·8	2·0104	0131	0158	0185	0212	0239	0266	0293	0319	0346	3	5	8	11	13	16	19	22	24
3·9	2·0373	0399	0426	0452	0478	0504	0531	0557	0583	0609	3	5	8	10	13	16	18	21	24
4·0	2·0634	0660	0686	0712	0737	0763	0788	0813	0839	0864	3	5	8	10	13	15	18	20	23
4·1	2·0889	0914	0939	0964	0989	1014	1039	1064	1088	1113	2	5	7	10	12	15	17	20	22
4·2	2·1137	1162	1186	1211	1235	1259	1283	1308	1332	1356	2	5	7	10	12	15	17	19	22
4·3	2·1380	1403	1427	1451	1475	1498	1522	1546	1569	1592	2	5	7	9	12	14	17	19	21
4·4	2·1616	1639	1662	1686	1709	1732	1755	1778	1801	1824	2	5	7	9	12	14	16	18	21
4·5	2·1846	1869	1892	1915	1937	1960	1982	2005	2027	2049	2	5	7	9	11	14	16	18	20
4·6	2·2072	2094	2116	2138	2160	2182	2204	2226	2248	2270	2	4	7	9	11	13	15	18	20
4·7	2·2292	2314	2335	2357	2379	2400	2422	2443	2465	2486	2	4	6	9	11	13	15	17	19
4·8	2·2507	2529	2550	2571	2592	2613	2634	2655	2676	2697	2	4	6	8	11	13	15	17	19
4·9	2·2718	2739	2760	2780	2801	2822	2842	2863	2883	2904	2	4	6	8	10	12	14	17	19
5·0	2·2924	2945	2965	2985	3006	3026	3046	3066	3086	3106	2	4	6	8	10	12	14	16	18
5·1	2·3126	3146	3166	3186	3206	3226	3246	3265	3285	3305	2	4	6	8	10	12	14	16	18
5·2	2·3324	3344	3363	3383	3402	3422	3441	3461	3480	3499	2	4	6	8	10	12	14	16	17
5·3	2·3518	3538	3557	3576	3595	3614	3633	3652	3671	3690	2	4	6	8	10	11	13	15	17
5·4	2·3709	3727	3746	3765	3784	3802	3821	3840	3858	3877	2	4	6	7	9	11	13	15	17

$$\cosh^{-1}x$$

x	0	1	2	3	4	5	6	7	8	9	1	2	3	4	5	6	7	8	9
5·5	2·3895	3914	3932	3951	3969	3987	4006	4024	4042	4060	2	4	6	7	9	11	13	15	17
5·6	2·4078	4097	4115	4133	4151	4169	4187	4205	4223	4240	2	4	5	7	9	11	13	14	16
5·7	2·4258	4276	4294	4312	4329	4347	4365	4382	4400	4417	2	4	5	7	9	11	12	14	16
5·8	2·4435	4452	4470	4487	4505	4522	4539	4557	4574	4591	2	3	5	7	9	10	12	14	16
5·9	2·4608	4626	4643	4660	4677	4694	4711	4728	4745	4762	2	3	5	7	9	10	12	14	15
6·0	2·4779	4796	4813	4829	4846	4863	4880	4897	4913	4930	2	3	5	7	8	10	12	13	15
6·1	2·4946	4963	4980	4996	5013	5029	5046	5062	5079	5095	2	3	5	7	8	10	12	13	15
6·2	2·5111	5128	5144	5160	5176	5193	5209	5225	5241	5257	2	3	5	6	8	10	11	13	15
6·3	2·5273	5289	5305	5321	5337	5353	5369	5385	5401	5417	2	3	5	6	8	10	11	13	14
6·4	2·5433	5449	5464	5480	5496	5512	5527	5543	5559	5574	2	3	5	6	8	9	11	13	14
6·5	2·5590	5605	5621	5636	5652	5667	5683	5698	5714	5729	2	3	5	6	8	9	11	12	14
6·6	2·5744	5760	5775	5790	5805	5821	5836	5851	5866	5881	2	3	5	6	8	9	11	12	14
6·7	2·5896	5911	5927	5942	5957	5972	5987	6001	6016	6031	1	3	4	6	7	9	10	12	13
6·8	2·6046	6061	6076	6091	6105	6120	6135	6150	6164	6179	1	3	4	6	7	9	10	12	13
6·9	2·6194	6208	6223	6238	6252	6267	6281	6296	6310	6325	1	3	4	6	7	9	10	12	13
7·0	2·6339	6354	6368	6382	6397	6411	6425	6440	6454	6468	1	3	4	6	7	9	10	11	13
7·1	2·6482	6497	6511	6525	6539	6553	6567	6582	6596	6610	1	3	4	6	7	8	10	11	13
7·2	2·6624	6638	6652	6666	6680	6694	6707	6721	6735	6749	1	3	4	6	7	8	10	11	13
7·3	2·6763	6777	6791	6804	6818	6832	6846	6859	6873	6887	1	3	4	5	7	8	10	11	12
7·4	2·6900	6914	6928	6941	6955	6968	6982	6995	7009	7022	1	3	4	5	7	8	9	11	12
7·5	2·7036	7049	7063	7076	7089	7103	7116	7129	7143	7156	1	3	4	5	7	8	9	11	12
7·6	2·7169	7183	7196	7209	7222	7236	7249	7262	7275	7288	1	3	4	5	7	8	9	11	12
7·7	2·7301	7314	7327	7340	7353	7367	7380	7393	7405	7418	1	3	4	5	7	8	9	10	12
7·8	2·7431	7444	7457	7470	7483	7496	7509	7521	7534	7547	1	3	4	5	6	8	9	10	12
7·9	2·7560	7573	7585	7598	7611	7623	7636	7649	7661	7674	1	3	4	5	6	8	9	10	11
8·0	2·7687	7699	7712	7724	7737	7749	7762	7774	7787	7799	1	3	4	5	6	8	9	10	11
8·1	2·7812	7824	7837	7849	7861	7874	7886	7898	7911	7923	1	2	4	5	6	7	9	10	11
8·2	2·7935	7948	7960	7972	7984	7997	8009	8021	8033	8045	1	2	4	5	6	7	9	10	11
8·3	2·8058	8070	8082	8094	8106	8118	8130	8142	8154	8166	1	2	4	5	6	7	8	10	11
8·4	2·8178	8190	8202	8214	8226	8238	8250	8262	8274	8285	1	2	4	5	6	7	8	10	11
8·5	2·8297	8309	8321	8333	8345	8356	8368	8380	8392	8403	1	2	4	5	6	7	8	9	11
8·6	2·8415	8427	8439	8450	8462	8473	8485	8497	8508	8520	1	2	3	5	6	7	8	9	10
8·7	2·8532	8543	8555	8566	8578	8589	8601	8612	8624	8635	1	2	3	5	6	7	8	9	10
8·8	2·8647	8658	8669	8681	8692	8704	8715	8726	8738	8749	1	2	3	5	6	7	8	9	10
8·9	2·8760	8772	8783	8794	8805	8817	8828	8839	8850	8862	1	2	3	5	6	7	8	9	10
9·0	2·8873	8884	8895	8906	8917	8928	8940	8951	8962	8973	1	2	3	4	6	7	8	9	10
9·1	2·8984	8995	9006	9017	9028	9039	9050	9061	9072	9083	1	2	3	4	6	7	8	9	10
9·2	2·9094	9105	9116	9127	9137	9148	9159	9170	9181	9192	1	2	3	4	5	7	8	9	10
9·3	2·9203	9213	9224	9235	9246	9257	9267	9278	9289	9299	1	2	3	4	5	6	8	9	10
9·4	2·9310	9321	9332	9342	9353	9364	9374	9385	9395	9406	1	2	3	4	5	6	7	9	10
9·5	2·9417	9427	9438	9448	9459	9469	9480	9490	9501	9511	1	2	3	4	5	6	7	8	9
9·6	2·9522	9532	9543	9553	9564	9574	9585	9595	9605	9616	1	2	3	4	5	6	7	8	9
9·7	2·9626	9636	9647	9657	9667	9678	9688	9698	9709	9719	1	2	3	4	5	6	7	8	9
9·8	2·9729	9739	9750	9760	9770	9780	9791	9801	9811	9821	1	2	3	4	5	6	7	8	9
9·9	2·9831	9841	9851	9862	9872	9882	9892	9902	9912	9922	1	2	3	4	5	6	7	8	9
10·0	2·9932	9942	9952	9962	9972	9982	9992	0002	0012	0022	1	2	3	4	5	6	7	8	9

Note: For values of x outside this range, use $\cosh^{-1}x = \ln\{x + \sqrt{(x^2 - 1)}\}$.

x	0	1	2	3	4	5	6	7	8	9	1	2	3	4	5	6	7	8	9
1·0	0·0000	0100	0198	0296	0392	0488	0583	0677	0770	0862	10	19	29	38	48	57	67	77	86
1·1	0·0953	1044	1133	1222	1310	1398	1484	1570	1655	1740	9	17	26	35	44	52	61	70	79
1·2	0·1823	1906	1989	2070	2151	2231	2311	2390	2469	2546	8	16	24	32	40	48	56	64	72
1·3	0·2624	2700	2776	2852	2927	3001	3075	3148	3221	3293	7	15	22	30	37	45	52	60	67
1·4	0·3365	3436	3507	3577	3646	3716	3784	3853	3920	3988	7	14	21	28	35	42	48	55	62
1·5	0·4055	4121	4187	4253	4318	4383	4447	4511	4574	4637	6	13	19	26	32	39	45	52	58
1·6	0·4700	4762	4824	4886	4947	5008	5068	5128	5188	5247	6	12	18	24	30	36	43	49	55
1·7	0·5306	5365	5423	5481	5539	5596	5653	5710	5766	5822	6	11	17	23	29	34	40	46	52
1·8	0·5878	5933	5988	6043	6098	6152	6206	6259	6313	6366	5	11	16	22	27	33	38	43	49
1·9	0·6419	6471	6523	6575	6627	6678	6729	6780	6831	6881	5	10	15	21	26	31	36	41	46
2·0	0·6931	6981	7031	7080	7129	7178	7227	7275	7324	7372	5	10	15	20	24	29	34	39	44
2·1	0·7419	7467	7514	7561	7608	7655	7701	7747	7793	7839	5	9	14	19	23	28	33	37	42
2·2	0·7885	7930	7975	8020	8065	8109	8154	8198	8242	8286	4	9	13	18	22	27	31	36	40
2·3	0·8329	8372	8416	8459	8502	8544	8587	8629	8671	8713	4	9	13	17	21	26	30	34	38
2·4	0·8755	8796	8838	8879	8920	8961	9002	9042	9083	9123	4	8	12	16	20	25	29	33	37
2·5	0·9163	9203	9243	9282	9322	9361	9400	9439	9478	9517	4	8	12	16	20	24	28	31	35
2·6	0·9555	9594	9632	9670	9708	9746	9783	9821	9858	9895	4	8	11	15	19	23	26	30	34
2·7	0·9933	9969	0006	0043	0080	0116	0152	0188	0225	0260	4	7	11	15	18	22	26	29	33
2·8	1·0296	0332	0367	0403	0438	0473	0508	0543	0578	0613	4	7	11	14	18	21	25	28	32
2·9	1·0647	0682	0716	0750	0784	0818	0852	0886	0919	0953	3	7	10	14	17	20	24	27	31
3·0	1·0986	1019	1053	1086	1119	1151	1184	1217	1249	1282	3	7	10	13	16	20	23	26	30
3·1	1·1314	1346	1378	1410	1442	1474	1506	1537	1569	1600	3	6	10	13	16	19	22	25	29
3·2	1·1632	1663	1694	1725	1756	1787	1817	1848	1878	1909	3	6	9	12	15	18	22	25	28
3·3	1·1939	1969	2000	2030	2060	2090	2119	2149	2179	2208	3	6	9	12	15	18	21	24	27
3·4	1·2238	2267	2296	2326	2355	2384	2413	2442	2470	2499	3	6	9	12	15	17	20	23	26
3·5	1·2528	2556	2585	2613	2641	2669	2698	2726	2754	2782	3	6	8	11	14	17	20	23	25
3·6	1·2809	2837	2865	2892	2920	2947	2975	3002	3029	3056	3	5	8	11	14	16	19	22	25
3·7	1·3083	3110	3137	3164	3191	3218	3244	3271	3297	3324	3	5	8	11	13	16	19	21	24
3·8	1·3350	3376	3403	3429	3455	3481	3507	3533	3558	3584	3	5	8	10	13	16	18	21	23
3·9	1·3610	3635	3661	3686	3712	3737	3762	3788	3813	3838	3	5	8	10	13	15	18	20	23
4·0	1·3863	3888	3913	3938	3962	3987	4012	4036	4061	4085	2	5	7	10	12	15	17	20	22
4·1	1·4110	4134	4159	4183	4207	4231	4255	4279	4303	4327	2	5	7	10	12	14	17	19	22
4·2	1·4351	4375	4398	4422	4446	4469	4493	4516	4540	4563	2	5	7	9	12	14	16	19	21
4·3	1·4586	4609	4633	4656	4679	4702	4725	4748	4770	4793	2	5	7	9	12	14	16	18	21
4·4	1·4816	4839	4861	4884	4907	4929	4951	4974	4996	5019	2	4	7	9	11	13	16	18	20
4·5	1·5041	5063	5085	5107	5129	5151	5173	5195	5217	5239	2	4	7	9	11	13	15	18	20
4·6	1·5261	5282	5304	5326	5347	5369	5390	5412	5433	5454	2	4	6	9	11	13	15	17	19
4·7	1·5476	5497	5518	5539	5560	5581	5602	5623	5644	5665	2	4	6	8	11	13	15	17	19
4·8	1·5686	5707	5728	5748	5769	5790	5810	5831	5851	5872	2	4	6	8	10	12	14	17	19
4·9	1·5892	5913	5933	5953	5974	5994	6014	6034	6054	6074	2	4	6	8	10	12	14	16	18
5·0	1·6094	6114	6134	6154	6174	6194	6214	6233	6253	6273	2	4	6	8	10	12	14	16	18
5·1	1·6292	6312	6332	6351	6371	6390	6409	6429	6448	6467	2	4	6	8	10	12	14	16	17
5·2	1·6487	6506	6525	6544	6563	6582	6601	6620	6639	6658	2	4	6	8	10	11	13	15	17
5·3	1·6677	6696	6715	6734	6752	6771	6790	6808	6827	6845	2	4	6	7	9	11	13	15	17

For further values, e.g. ln 4560, write $4560 = 4\cdot560 \times 10^3$, so that $\ln 4560 = \ln 4\cdot560 + \ln 10^3$ and use the table below.

x	1	2	3	4	5	6
$\ln 10^x$	2·3026	4·6052	6·9078	9·2103	11·5129	13·8155

NATURAL LOGARITHMS (ln x)

x	0	1	2	3	4	5	6	7	8	9	1	2	3	4	5	6	7	8	9
5·4	1·6864	6882	6901	6919	6938	6956	6974	6993	7011	7029	2	4	6	7	9	11	13	15	17
5·5	1·7047	7066	7084	7102	7120	7138	7156	7174	7192	7210	2	4	5	7	9	11	13	14	16
5·6	1·7228	7246	7263	7281	7299	7317	7334	7352	7370	7387	2	4	5	7	9	11	12	14	16
5·7	1·7405	7422	7440	7457	7475	7492	7509	7527	7544	7561	2	3	5	7	9	10	12	14	16
5·8	1·7579	7596	7613	7630	7647	7664	7681	7699	7716	7733	2	3	5	7	9	10	12	14	15
5·9	1·7750	7766	7783	7800	7817	7834	7851	7867	7884	7901	2	3	5	7	8	10	12	13	15
6·0	1·7918	7934	7951	7967	7984	8001	8017	8034	8050	8066	2	3	5	7	8	10	12	13	15
6·1	1·8083	8099	8116	8132	8148	8165	8181	8197	8213	8229	2	3	5	7	8	10	11	13	15
6·2	1·8245	8262	8278	8294	8310	8326	8342	8358	8374	8390	2	3	5	6	8	10	11	13	14
6·3	1·8405	8421	8437	8453	8469	8485	8500	8516	8532	8547	2	3	5	6	8	9	11	13	14
6·4	1·8563	8579	8594	8610	8625	8641	8656	8672	8687	8703	2	3	5	6	8	9	11	12	14
6·5	1·8718	8733	8749	8764	8779	8795	8810	8825	8840	8856	2	3	5	6	8	9	11	12	14
6·6	1·8871	8886	8901	8916	8931	8946	8961	8976	8991	9006	2	3	5	6	8	9	11	12	14
6·7	1·9021	9036	9051	9066	9081	9095	9110	9125	9140	9155	1	3	4	6	7	9	10	12	13
6·8	1·9169	9184	9199	9213	9228	9242	9257	9272	9286	9301	1	3	4	6	7	9	10	12	13
6·9	1·9315	9330	9344	9359	9373	9387	9402	9416	9430	9445	1	3	4	6	7	9	10	12	13
7·0	1·9459	9473	9488	9502	9516	9530	9544	9559	9573	9587	1	3	4	6	7	9	10	11	13
7·1	1·9601	9615	9629	9643	9657	9671	9685	9699	9713	9727	1	3	4	6	7	8	10	11	13
7·2	1·9741	9755	9769	9782	9796	9810	9824	9838	9851	9865	1	3	4	6	7	8	10	11	12
7·3	1·9879	9892	9906	9920	9933	9947	9961	9974	9988	0001	1	3	4	5	7	8	10	11	12
7·4	2·0015	0028	0042	0055	0069	0082	0096	0109	0122	0136	1	3	4	5	7	8	9	11	12
7·5	2·0149	0162	0176	0189	0202	0215	0229	0242	0255	0268	1	3	4	5	7	8	9	11	12
7·6	2·0281	0295	0308	0321	0334	0347	0360	0373	0386	0399	1	3	4	5	7	8	9	10	12
7·7	2·0412	0425	0438	0451	0464	0477	0490	0503	0516	0528	1	3	4	5	6	8	9	10	12
7·8	2·0541	0554	0567	0580	0592	0605	0618	0631	0643	0656	1	3	4	5	6	8	9	10	11
7·9	2·0669	0681	0694	0707	0719	0732	0744	0757	0769	0782	1	3	4	5	6	8	9	10	11
8·0	2·0794	0807	0819	0832	0844	0857	0869	0882	0894	0906	1	2	4	5	6	7	9	10	11
8·1	2·0919	0931	0943	0956	0968	0980	0992	1005	1017	1029	1	2	4	5	6	7	9	10	11
8·2	2·1041	1054	1066	1078	1090	1102	1114	1126	1138	1150	1	2	4	5	6	7	8	10	11
8·3	2·1163	1175	1187	1199	1211	1223	1235	1247	1258	1270	1	2	4	5	6	7	8	10	11
8·4	2·1282	1294	1306	1318	1330	1342	1353	1365	1377	1389	1	2	4	5	6	7	8	9	11
8·5	2·1401	1412	1424	1436	1448	1459	1471	1483	1494	1506	1	2	4	5	6	7	8	9	11
8·6	2·1518	1529	1541	1552	1564	1576	1587	1599	1610	1622	1	2	3	5	6	7	8	9	10
8·7	2·1633	1645	1656	1668	1679	1691	1702	1713	1725	1736	1	2	3	5	6	7	8	9	10
8·8	2·1748	1759	1770	1782	1793	1804	1815	1827	1838	1849	1	2	3	5	6	7	8	9	10
8·9	2·1861	1872	1883	1894	1905	1917	1928	1939	1950	1961	1	2	3	4	6	7	8	9	10
9·0	2·1972	1983	1994	2006	2017	2028	2039	2050	2061	2072	1	2	3	4	6	7	8	9	10
9·1	2·2083	2094	2105	2116	2127	2138	2148	2159	2170	2181	1	2	3	4	5	7	8	9	10
9·2	2·2192	2203	2214	2225	2235	2246	2257	2268	2279	2289	1	2	3	4	5	6	8	9	10
9·3	2·2300	2311	2322	2332	2343	2354	2364	2375	2386	2396	1	2	3	4	5	6	7	9	10
9·4	2·2407	2418	2428	2439	2450	2460	2471	2481	2492	2502	1	2	3	4	5	6	7	8	10
9·5	2·2513	2523	2534	2544	2555	2565	2576	2586	2597	2607	1	2	3	4	5	6	7	8	9
9·6	2·2618	2628	2638	2649	2659	2670	2680	2690	2701	2711	1	2	3	4	5	6	7	8	9
9·7	2·2721	2732	2742	2752	2762	2773	2783	2793	2803	2814	1	2	3	4	5	6	7	8	9
9·8	2·2824	2834	2844	2854	2865	2875	2885	2895	2905	2915	1	2	3	4	5	6	7	8	9
9·9	2·2925	2935	2946	2956	2966	2976	2986	2996	3006	3016	1	2	3	4	5	6	7	8	9

NORMAL PROBABILITY TABLES

Table of φ(x)

x	$\phi(x)$	x	$\phi(x)$	x	$\phi(x)$	x	$\phi(x)$
0·0	·399	0·8	·290	1·6	·111	2·4	·022
0·1	·397	0·9	·266	1·7	·094	2·5	·018
0·2	·391	1·0	·242	1·8	·079	2·6	·014
0·3	·381	1·1	·218	1·9	·066	2·7	·010
0·4	·368	1·2	·194	2·0	·054	2·8	·008
0·5	·352	1·3	·171	2·1	·044	2·9	·006
0·6	·333	1·4	·150	2·2	·035	3 0	·004
0·7	·312	1·5	·130	2·3	·028		

Table of Φ(x)

x	0	1	2	3	4	5	6	7	8	9
0·0	·500	·504	·508	·512	·516	·520	·524	·528	·532	·536
0·1	·540	·544	·548	·552	·556	·560	·564	·567	·571	·575
0·2	·579	·583	·587	·591	·595	·599	·603	·606	·610	·614
0·3	·618	·622	·626	·629	·633	·637	·641	·644	·648	·652
0·4	·655	·659	·663	·666	·670	·674	·677	·681	·684	·688
0·5	·691	·695	·698	·702	·705	·709	·712	·716	·719	·722
0·6	·726	·729	·732	·736	·739	·742	·745	·749	·752	·755
0·7	·758	·761	·764	·767	·770	·773	·776	·779	·782	·785
0·8	·788	·791	·794	·797	·800	·802	·805	·808	·811	·813
0·9	·816	·819	·821	·824	·826	·829	·831	·834	·836	·839
1·0	·841	·844	·846	·848	·851	·853	·855	·858	·860	·862
1·1	·864	·867	·869	·871	·873	·875	·877	·879	·881	·883
1·2	·885	·887	·889	·891	·893	·894	·896	·898	·900	·901
1·3	·903	·905	·907	·908	·910	·911	·913	·915	·916	·918
1·4	·919	·921	·922	·924	·925	·926	·928	·929	·931	·932
1·5	·933	·934	·936	·937	·938	·939	·941	·942	·943	·944
1·6	·945	·946	·947	·948	·949	·951	·952	·953	·954	·954
1·7	·955	·956	·957	·958	·959	·960	·961	·962	·962	·963
1·8	·964	·965	·966	·966	·967	·968	·969	·969	·970	·971
1·9	·971	·972	·973	·973	·974	·974	·975	·976	·976	·977
2·0	·977	·978	·978	·979	·979	·980	·980	·981	·981	·982
2·1	·982	·983	·983	·983	·984	·984	·985	·985	·985	·986
2·2	·986	·986	·987	·987	·987	·988	·988	·988	·989	·989
2·3	·989	·990	·990	·990	·990	·991	·991	·991	·991	·992
2·4	·992	·992	·992	·992	·993	·993	·993	·993	·993	·994
2·5	·994	·994	·994	·994	·994	·995	·995	·995	·995	·995
2·6	·995	·995	·996	·996	·996	·996	·996	·996	·996	·996
2·7	·996	·997	·997	·997	·997	·997	·997	·997	·997	·997
2·8	·997	·997	·997	·997	·997	·997	·997	·998	·998	·998
2·9	·998	·998	·998	·998	·998	·998	·999	·999	·999	·999
3·0	·999	·999	·999	·999	·999	·999	·999	·999	·999	·999

The functions tabulated are

$$\phi(x) = \frac{1}{\sqrt{(2\pi)}}\, e^{-\frac{1}{2}x^2} \quad \text{and} \quad \Phi(x) = \int_{-\infty}^{x} \phi(t)\, dt.$$

$\phi(x)$ is the ordinate of the Normal frequency curve. $\Phi(x)$ is the probability that a random variable having a Normal frequency density, with zero mean and unit variance, will be less than x.

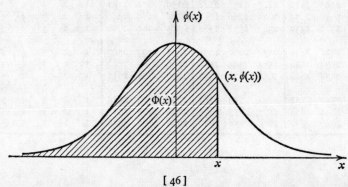

χ^2 PROBABILITY DENSITY FUNCTION

P	99	95	10	5	1	0·1
$\nu = 1$	0·000157	0·00393	2·71	3·84	6·64	10·83
2	0·0201	0·102	4·61	5·99	9·21	13·75
3	0·115	0·352	6·25	7·81	11·34	16·27
4	0·297	0·711	7·78	9·49	13·28	18·47
5	0·554	1·15	9·24	11·07	15·09	20·51
6	0·873	1·64	10·64	12·59	16·81	22·46
7	1·24	2·17	12·02	14·07	18·47	24·32
8	1·65	2·73	13·36	15·51	20·09	26·12
9	2·09	3·33	14·68	16·92	21·67	27·88
10	2·56	3·94	15·99	18·31	23·21	29·59
11	3·05	4·57	17·27	19·68	24·72	31·26
12	3·57	5·23	18·55	21·03	26·21	32·91
13	4·11	5·89	19·81	22·36	27·69	34·53
14	4·66	6·57	21·06	23·68	29·14	36·12
15	5·23	7·26	22·31	25·00	30·58	37·70
20	8·26	10·85	28·41	31·41	37·57	45·31
30	14·96	18·49	40·26	43·77	50·89	59·66
40	22·17	26·51	51·81	55·76	63·69	73·40
50	29·71	34·76	63·17	67·50	76·15	86·68
60	37·49	43·19	74·40	79·08	88·38	99·72

The function tabulated is χ_P^2 defined by

$$\frac{P}{100} = \frac{\int_{\chi_P^2}^{\infty} x^{\frac{1}{2}\nu-1} e^{-\frac{1}{2}x} dx}{\int_0^{\infty} x^{\frac{1}{2}\nu-1} e^{-\frac{1}{2}x} dx}.$$

If x is a random variable with probability density function that of χ^2 with ν degrees of freedom then $P/100$ is the probability that $x \geqslant \chi_P^2$.

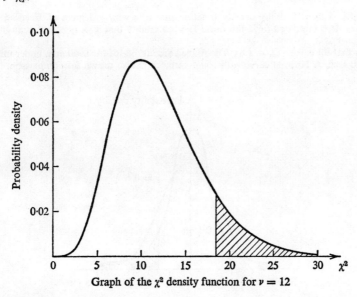

Graph of the χ^2 density function for $\nu = 12$

The graph illustrates that for $\nu = 12$, $\chi_{10}^2 = 18·55$. The shaded area is $\frac{10}{100}$ of the total.

For $10 < \nu < 70$ linear interpolation or extrapolation in ν is adequate. The percentage accuracy is better for small P than large P and for large ν than small ν.

Example. To estimate χ_P^2 for $\nu = 70$, $P = 10$.

The difference between χ_{10}^2 for $\nu = 50$ and $\nu = 60$ is 11·23. Our estimate is $\chi_{10}^2 = 85·63$. (The correct value is 85·53.)

[47]

P	20	10	5	2	1	0·2	0·1
ν = 1	3·08	6·31	12·7	31·8	63·7	318	637
2	1·89	2·92	4·30	6·96	9·93	22·3	31·6
3	1·64	2·35	3·18	4·54	5·84	10·2	12·9
4	1·53	2·13	2·78	3·75	4·60	7·18	8·61
5	1·48	2·02	2·57	3·36	4·03	5·89	6·87
6	1·44	1·94	2·45	3·14	3·71	5·21	5·96
7	1·41	1·89	2·36	3·00	3·50	4·78	5·41
8	1·40	1·86	2·31	2·90	3·36	4·50	5·04
9	1·38	1·83	2·26	2·82	3·25	4·29	4·78
10	1·37	1·81	2·23	2·76	3·17	4·15	4·58
11	1·36	1·80	2·20	2·72	3·11	4·02	4·44
12	1·36	1·78	2·18	2·68	3·05	3·93	4·32
13	1·35	1·77	2·16	2·65	3·01	3·85	4·22
14	1·35	1·76	2·14	2·62	2·98	3·79	4·14
15	1·34	1·75	2·13	2·60	2·95	3·73	4·07
20	1·33	1·72	2·09	2·53	2·85	3·55	3·85
30	1·31	1·70	2·04	2·46	2·75	3·38	3·64
40	1·30	1·68	2·02	2·42	2·70	3·31	3·55
50	1·30	1·68	2·01	2·40	2·68	3·26	3·50
60	1·30	1·67	2·00	2·39	2·66	3·23	3·46
∞	1·28	1·64	1·96	2·33	2·58	3·09	3·29

The values for $\nu = \infty$ are those from a Normal probability function, which is the limiting form for large ν.

The function tabulated is t_P, defined by

$$\frac{P}{100} = \frac{\int_{t_P}^{\infty} \left(1 + \frac{t^2}{\nu}\right)^{-\frac{1}{2}(\nu+1)} dt}{\int_0^{\infty} \left(1 + \frac{t^2}{\nu}\right)^{-\frac{1}{2}(\nu+1)} dt}.$$

If x is a random variable with probability density function that of t with ν degrees of freedom then $P/100$ is the probability that $|x| \geqslant t_P$. It is tabulated for 2-tail tests. The probability that $x \geqslant t_P$ is half that given at the head of the table.

The graph illustrates that for $\nu = 4$, $t_{20} = 1·63$. The shaded area is $\frac{20}{100}$ of the total area under the bold graph. Each tail contains $\frac{10}{100}$ of the area. A Normal curve with equal variance is also drawn for comparison.

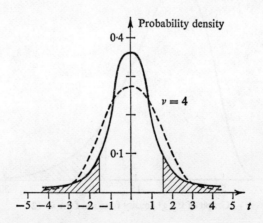

For $\nu > 10$ linear interpolation in $120/\nu$ is adequate. The percentage accuracy is better for large P than small P and for large ν than small ν.

Example. To estimate t_P for $\nu = 16$, $P = 2$.

Take $t_2 = 2·60$ for $\nu = 15$; $t_2 = 2·53$ for $\nu = 20$. The values of $120/\nu$ are 8, $7\frac{1}{2}$ and 6 so that the required difference is $\frac{1}{4} \times ·07$, then $t_2 \approx 2·58$ for $\nu = 16$ (accurate to 3 S.F.).

89 90	26 36	22 74	71 13	74 05	58 67	79 59	34 69	67 51	58 57	76 58	17 38
86 38	25 76	20 69	35 84	53 73	47 38	46 54	91 63	33 65	25 02	32 03	66 23
98 10	31 80	82 41	41 82	54 76	90 22	95 78	25 58	06 68	19 49	08 95	74 83
94 18	87 43	71 84	45 45	96 43	59 63	23 13	54 79	61 67	36 37	33 26	87 75
33 69	26 21	93 49	56 64	25 68	49 58	90 47	33 17	19 56	33 36	11 72	19 09
85 71	59 36	22 42	88 11	63 09	63 24	95 76	07 89	89 07	73 09	74 88	23 55
32 25	01 53	36 19	10 42	49 50	98 75	38 88	65 44	00 45	88 37	41 62	84 72
17 85	78 43	44 60	69 05	86 59	66 98	92 56	79 88	70 45	05 62	17 74	81 88
04 50	22 00	74 57	49 82	75 34	25 90	05 50	24 63	30 64	31 84	66 19	83 47
79 91	04 95	34 45	08 62	83 99	81 26	89 40	61 49	94 30	94 66	08 26	10 42
48 01	83 62	70 23	81 29	23 84	38 91	91 50	19 93	25 54	61 74	26 05	34 65
95 14	63 02	09 68	89 66	32 52	16 05	39 39	02 71	55 99	16 45	98 67	01 58
58 51	58 85	13 72	52 57	84 58	66 68	32 58	66 07	78 74	03 42	81 93	73 32
88 50	46 86	70 24	86 62	38 78	33 76	68 20	67 61	29 72	52 17	44 56	96 53
16 54	05 64	73 80	20 83	44 09	66 51	28 72	97 48	68 60	20 96	55 47	55 73
20 73	33 39	25 44	19 13	68 71	26 81	25 14	30 75	74 61	56 70	93 47	12 50
47 38	74 44	92 47	37 84	03 89	26 23	52 41	06 59	38 43	03 46	88 95	91 96
58 17	60 57	02 99	45 72	45 42	61 47	15 18	73 12	98 26	83 31	83 99	24 07
26 81	50 42	24 97	87 14	89 71	83 17	14 93	46 12	16 74	95 10	99 87	21 05
95 64	20 88	42 63	17 25	80 41	33 22	25 83	65 08	33 05	89 61	29 86	12 19
29 80	09 62	33 60	64 44	31 22	31 70	18 11	07 85	70 74	91 17	91 45	76 77
70 46	91 35	07 77	27 84	40 20	77 25	44 00	03 23	45 60	02 22	61 67	08 49
96 67	06 01	60 64	69 46	17 69	27 55	98 32	05 66	88 46	68 25	87 25	14 16
12 25	05 68	84 84	62 91	23 97	99 19	93 94	66 51	22 45	41 59	66 80	62 63
18 65	57 35	74 25	81 35	62 62	01 43	74 05	88 51	53 69	88 78	15 71	96 11
52 49	40 62	32 80	98 03	42 14	61 02	77 11	87 66	70 56	20 35	02 91	51 30
13 62	74 91	12 44	96 86	45 98	55 33	06 71	98 91	20 22	29 56	66 82	80 02
33 31	40 35	41 32	48 21	85 70	71 89	76 31	87 22	55 58	90 72	39 82	53 69
80 77	73 73	18 15	96 48	26 00	60 98	89 18	07 71	62 39	86 97	15 97	09 82
69 82	64 04	67 28	95 36	60 92	32 00	68 83	62 23	32 55	61 16	94 01	09 82
31 08	33 58	06 53	24 59	05 09	42 83	67 73	48 81	85 62	92 49	25 93	56 45
58 11	60 05	86 12	24 52	89 45	93 31	15 87	94 84	90 03	64 06	15 63	01 73
68 32	40 38	37 45	39 99	26 02	59 97	12 64	67 43	86 80	14 45	60 08	12 08
22 45	63 38	51 44	94 68	48 49	56 06	09 22	52 95	50 13	84 46	80 27	65 93
00 38	56 12	37 21	19 81	02 72	75 49	44 41	24 66	55 22	60 79	80 97	83 06
84 76	13 46	00 67	48 58	42 75	77 04	97 19	66 07	55 66	38 61	68 17	66 99
97 80	90 05	58 62	97 03	58 03	05 59	38 74	54 95	87 04	59 87	81 07	67 94
26 86	92 06	77 04	10 51	91 26	24 43	94 89	39 62	88 72	11 52	66 47	51 79
39 24	80 25	00 41	97 85	59 58	63 97	89 09	22 21	11 86	51 18	33 08	95 67
66 58	86 48	27 66	78 53	22 51	25 31	87 95	74 75	50 04	42 05	71 92	13 15
73 64	76 36	02 06	33 96	35 22	85 86	96 30	00 18	05 37	41 90	85 50	99 13
85 23	58 50	31 15	30 82	44 92	72 55	58 59	98 92	39 34	60 94	48 68	85 58
53 10	34 43	02 07	65 97	57 25	39 09	15 69	67 79	91 75	71 27	95 74	86 20
53 58	40 68	34 29	94 10	07 42	07 22	17 24	36 42	59 05	70 19	07 71	88 72
45 40	02 88	03 70	75 11	91 74	11 68	56 39	86 08	00 73	41 56	39 75	89 50
61 72	39 11	34 39	68 80	08 81	64 23	74 68	28 94	02 59	82 22	55 39	51 19
84 30	20 34	25 31	26 51	65 21	77 37	79 33	53 47	79 02	51 78	79 17	66 05
34 07	51 42	92 86	47 09	52 90	94 27	47 73	55 39	38 62	93 20	92 75	38 53
20 59	05 44	83 29	01 98	88 06	51 48	45 38	63 98	41 93	87 79	18 13	31 90
29 87	94 10	13 43	59 63	45 98	29 97	26 55	46 21	42 55	02 07	06 05	95 88

This table produces sequences of digits 0 to 9 in an order which may be used to simulate the drawing of digits from a population in which each has a probability of $\frac{1}{10}$. Any pattern of positions in the table (such as reading the second digits of the pairs in the third column) may be used, provided it is decided in advance of looking at the table, and that it does not depend on the digits previously noted. A random sequence of digits 1 to 6 each with probability $\frac{1}{6}$ may, of course, be got by proceeding as before and ignoring the unwanted digits. A random sequence of digits 0 and 1 with probabilities $\frac{2}{3}$ and $\frac{1}{3}$ can be simulated by mapping 0 to 5 on to 0 and 6 to 8 on to 1, ignoring 9. Other uses can be devised as required.

SQUARES

	0	1	2	3	4	5	6	7	8	9	1	2	3	4	5	6	7	8	9
1.0	1.000	1.020	1.040	1.061	1.082	1.102	1.124	1.145	1.166	1.188	2	4	6	8	10	13	15	17	19
1.1	1.210	1.232	1.254	1.277	1.300	1.322	1.346	1.369	1.392	1.416	2	5	7	9	11	14	16	18	21
1.2	1.440	1.464	1.488	1.513	1.538	1.562	1.588	1.613	1.638	1.664	2	5	7	10	12	15	17	20	22
1.3	1.690	1.716	1.742	1.769	1.796	1.822	1.850	1.877	1.904	1.932	3	5	8	11	13	16	19	22	24
1.4	1.960	1.988	2.016	2.045	2.074	2.102	2.132	2.161	2.190	2.220	3	6	9	12	14	17	20	23	26
1.5	2.250	2.280	2.310	2.341	2.372	2.402	2.434	2.465	2.496	2.528	3	6	9	12	15	19	22	25	28
1.6	2.560	2.592	2.624	2.657	2.690	2.722	2.756	2.789	2.822	2.856	3	7	10	13	16	20	23	26	30
1.7	2.890	2.924	2.958	2.993	3.028	3.062	3.098	3.133	3.168	3.204	3	7	10	14	17	21	24	28	31
1.8	3.240	3.276	3.312	3.349	3.386	3.422	3.460	3.497	3.534	3.572	4	7	11	15	18	22	26	30	33
1.9	3.610	3.648	3.686	3.725	3.764	3.802	3.842	3.881	3.920	3.960	4	8	12	16	19	23	27	31	35
2.0	4.000	4.040	4.080	4.121	4.162	4.202	4.244	4.285	4.326	4.368	4	8	12	16	20	25	29	33	37
2.1	4.410	4.452	4.494	4.537	4.580	4.622	4.666	4.709	4.752	4.796	4	9	13	17	21	26	30	34	39
2.2	4.840	4.884	4.928	4.973	5.018	5.062	5.108	5.153	5.198	5.244	4	9	13	18	22	27	31	36	40
2.3	5.290	5.336	5.382	5.429	5.476	5.522	5.570	5.617	5.664	5.712	5	9	14	19	23	28	33	38	42
2.4	5.760	5.808	5.856	5.905	5.954	6.002	6.052	6.101	6.150	6.200	5	10	15	20	24	29	34	39	44
2.5	6.250	6.300	6.350	6.401	6.452	6.502	6.554	6.605	6.656	6.708	5	10	15	20	25	31	36	41	46
2.6	6.760	6.812	6.864	6.917	6.970	7.022	7.076	7.129	7.182	7.236	5	11	16	21	26	32	37	42	48
2.7	7.290	7.344	7.398	7.453	7.508	7.562	7.618	7.673	7.728	7.784	5	11	16	22	27	33	38	44	49
2.8	7.840	7.896	7.952	8.009	8.066	8.122	8.180	8.237	8.294	8.352	6	11	17	23	28	34	40	46	51
2.9	8.410	8.468	8.526	8.585	8.644	8.702	8.762	8.821	8.880	8.940	6	12	18	24	29	35	41	47	53
3.0	9.000	9.060	9.120	9.181	9.242	9.302	9.364	9.425	9.486	9.548	6	12	18	24	30	37	43	49	55
3.1	9.610	9.672	9.734	9.797	9.860	9.922	9.986	10.049	10.112	10.176	6	13	19	25	31	38	44	50	57
3.2	10.240	10.304	10.368	10.433	10.498	10.562	10.628	10.693	10.758	10.824	6	13	19	26	32	39	45	52	58
3.3	10.890	10.956	11.022	11.089	11.156	11.222	11.290	11.357	11.424	11.492	7	13	20	27	33	40	47	54	60
3.4	11.560	11.628	11.696	11.765	11.834	11.902	11.972	12.041	12.110	12.180	7	14	21	28	34	41	48	55	62
3.5	12.250	12.320	12.390	12.461	12.532	12.602	12.674	12.745	12.816	12.888	7	14	21	28	35	43	50	57	64
3.6	12.960	13.032	13.104	13.177	13.250	13.322	13.396	13.469	13.542	13.616	7	15	22	29	36	44	51	58	66
3.7	13.690	13.764	13.838	13.913	13.988	14.062	14.138	14.213	14.288	14.364	7	15	22	30	37	45	52	60	67
3.8	14.440	14.516	14.592	14.669	14.746	14.822	14.900	14.977	15.054	15.132	8	15	23	31	38	46	54	62	69
3.9	15.210	15.288	15.366	15.445	15.524	15.602	15.682	15.761	15.840	15.920	8	16	24	32	39	47	55	63	71
4.0	16.000	16.080	16.160	16.241	16.322	16.402	16.484	16.565	16.646	16.728	8	16	24	32	40	49	57	65	73
4.1	16.810	16.892	16.974	17.057	17.140	17.222	17.306	17.389	17.472	17.556	8	17	25	33	41	50	58	66	75
4.2	17.640	17.724	17.808	17.893	17.978	18.062	18.148	18.233	18.318	18.404	8	17	25	34	42	51	59	68	76
4.3	18.490	18.576	18.662	18.749	18.836	18.922	19.010	19.097	19.184	19.272	9	17	26	35	43	52	61	70	78
4.4	19.360	19.448	19.536	19.625	19.714	19.802	19.892	19.981	20.070	20.160	9	18	27	36	44	53	62	71	80
4.5	20.250	20.340	20.430	20.521	20.612	20.702	20.794	20.885	20.976	21.068	9	18	27	36	45	55	64	73	82
4.6	21.160	21.252	21.344	21.437	21.530	21.622	21.716	21.809	21.902	21.996	9	19	28	37	46	56	65	74	84
4.7	22.090	22.184	22.278	22.373	22.468	22.562	22.658	22.753	22.848	22.944	9	19	28	38	47	57	66	76	85
4.8	23.040	23.136	23.232	23.329	23.426	23.522	23.620	23.717	23.814	23.912	10	19	29	39	48	58	68	78	87
4.9	24.010	24.108	24.206	24.305	24.404	24.502	24.602	24.701	24.800	24.900	10	20	30	40	49	59	69	79	89
5.0	25.000	25.100	25.200	25.301	25.402	25.502	25.604	25.705	25.806	25.908	10	20	30	40	50	61	71	81	91
5.1	26.010	26.112	26.214	26.317	26.420	26.522	26.626	26.729	26.832	26.936	10	21	31	41	51	62	72	82	93
5.2	27.040	27.144	27.248	27.353	27.458	27.562	27.668	27.773	27.878	27.984	10	21	31	42	52	63	73	84	94
5.3	28.090	28.196	28.302	28.409	28.516	28.622	28.730	28.837	28.944	29.052	11	21	32	43	53	64	75	86	96
5.4	29.160	29.268	29.376	29.485	29.594	29.702	29.812	29.921	30.030	30.140	11	22	33	44	54	65	76	87	98

SQUARES

	0	1	2	3	4	5	6	7	8	9	1	2	3	4	5	6	7	8	9
5·5	30·25	30·36	30·47	30·58	30·69	30·80	30·91	31·02	31·14	31·25	1	2	3	4	6	7	8	9	10
5·6	31·36	31·47	31·58	31·70	31·81	31·92	32·04	32·15	32·26	32·38	1	2	3	5	6	7	8	9	10
5·7	32·49	32·60	32·72	32·83	32·95	33·06	33·18	33·29	33·41	33·52	1	2	3	5	6	7	8	9	10
5·8	33·64	33·76	33·87	33·99	34·11	34·22	34·34	34·46	34·57	34·69	1	2	4	5	6	7	8	9	11
5·9	34·81	34·93	35·05	35·16	35·28	35·40	35·52	35·64	35·76	35·88	1	2	4	5	6	7	8	10	11
6·0	36·00	36·12	36·24	36·36	36·48	36·60	36·72	36·84	36·97	37·09	1	2	4	5	6	7	8	10	11
6·1	37·21	37·33	37·45	37·58	37·70	37·82	37·95	38·07	38·19	38·32	1	2	4	5	6	7	9	10	11
6·2	38·44	38·56	38·69	38·81	38·94	39·06	39·19	39·31	39·44	39·56	1	2	4	5	6	7	9	10	11
6·3	39·69	39·82	39·94	40·07	40·20	40·32	40·45	40·58	40·70	40·83	1	3	4	5	6	8	9	10	11
6·4	40·96	41·09	41·22	41·34	41·47	41·60	41·73	41·86	41·99	42·12	1	3	4	5	6	8	9	10	12
6·5	42·25	42·38	42·51	42·64	42·77	42·90	43·03	43·16	43·30	43·43	1	3	4	5	7	8	9	10	12
6·6	43·56	43·69	43·82	43·96	44·09	44·22	44·36	44·49	44·62	44·76	1	3	4	5	7	8	9	11	12
6·7	44·89	45·02	45·16	45·29	45·43	45·56	45·70	45·83	45·97	46·10	1	3	4	5	7	8	9	11	12
6·8	46·24	46·38	46·51	46·65	46·79	46·92	47·06	47·20	47·33	47·47	1	3	4	5	7	8	10	11	12
6·9	47·61	47·75	47·89	48·02	48·16	48·30	48·44	48·58	48·72	48·86	1	3	4	6	7	8	10	11	13
7·0	49·00	49·14	49·28	49·42	49·56	49·70	49·84	49·98	50·13	50·27	1	3	4	6	7	8	10	11	13
7·1	50·41	50·55	50·69	50·84	50·98	51·12	51·27	51·41	51·55	51·70	1	3	4	6	7	9	10	11	13
7·2	51·84	51·98	52·13	52·27	52·42	52·56	52·71	52·85	53·00	53·14	1	3	4	6	7	9	10	12	13
7·3	53·29	53·44	53·58	53·73	53·88	54·02	54·17	54·32	54·46	54·61	1	3	4	6	7	9	10	12	13
7·4	54·76	54·91	55·06	55·20	55·35	55·50	55·65	55·80	55·95	56·10	1	3	4	6	7	9	10	12	13
7·5	56·25	56·40	56·55	56·70	56·85	57·00	57·15	57·30	57·46	57·61	2	3	5	6	8	9	11	12	14
7·6	57·76	57·91	58·06	58·22	58·37	58·52	58·68	58·83	58·98	59·14	2	3	5	6	8	9	11	12	14
7·7	59·29	59·44	59·60	59·75	59·91	60·06	60·22	60·37	60·53	60·68	2	3	5	6	8	9	11	12	14
7·8	60·84	61·00	61·15	61·31	61·47	61·62	61·78	61·94	62·09	62·25	2	3	5	6	8	9	11	13	14
7·9	62·41	62·57	62·73	62·88	63·04	63·20	63·36	63·52	63·68	63·84	2	3	5	6	8	10	11	13	14
8·0	64·00	64·16	64·32	64·48	64·64	64·80	64·96	65·12	65·29	65·45	2	3	5	6	8	10	11	13	14
8·1	65·61	65·77	65·93	66·10	66·26	66·42	66·59	66·75	66·91	67·08	2	3	5	7	8	10	11	13	15
8·2	67·24	67·40	67·57	67·73	67·90	68·06	68·23	68·39	68·56	68·72	2	3	5	7	8	10	12	13	15
8·3	68·89	69·06	69·22	69·39	69·56	69·72	69·89	70·06	70·22	70·39	2	3	5	7	8	10	12	13	15
8·4	70·56	70·73	70·90	71·06	71·23	71·40	71·57	71·74	71·91	72·08	2	3	5	7	8	10	12	14	15
8·5	72·25	72·42	72·59	72·76	72·93	73·10	73·27	73·44	73·62	73·79	2	3	5	7	9	10	12	14	15
8·6	73·96	74·13	74·30	74·48	74·65	74·82	75·00	75·17	75·34	75·52	2	3	5	7	9	10	12	14	16
8·7	75·69	75·86	76·04	76·21	76·39	76·56	76·74	76·91	77·09	77·26	2	3	5	7	9	10	12	14	16
8·8	77·44	77·62	77·79	77·97	78·15	78·32	78·50	78·68	78·85	79·03	2	4	5	7	9	11	12	14	16
8·9	79·21	79·39	79·57	79·74	79·92	80·10	80·28	80·46	80·64	80·82	2	4	5	7	9	11	13	14	16
9·0	81·00	81·18	81·36	81·54	81·72	81·90	82·08	82·26	82·45	82·63	2	4	5	7	9	11	13	14	16
9·1	82·81	82·99	83·17	83·36	83·54	83·72	83·91	84·09	84·27	84·46	2	4	5	7	9	11	13	15	16
9·2	84·64	84·82	85·01	85·19	85·38	85·56	85·75	85·93	86·12	86·30	2	4	6	7	9	11	13	15	17
9·3	86·49	86·68	86·86	87·05	87·24	87·42	87·61	87·80	87·98	88·17	2	4	6	7	9	11	13	15	17
9·4	88·36	88·55	88·74	88·92	89·11	89·30	89·49	89·68	89·87	90·06	2	4	6	8	9	11	13	15	17
9·5	90·25	90·44	90·63	90·82	91·01	91·20	91·39	91·58	91·78	91·97	2	4	6	8	10	11	13	15	17
9·6	92·16	92·35	92·54	92·74	92·93	93·12	93·32	93·51	93·70	93·90	2	4	6	8	10	12	14	15	17
9·7	94·09	94·28	94·48	94·67	94·87	95·06	95·26	95·45	95·65	95·84	2	4	6	8	10	12	14	16	18
9·8	96·04	96·24	96·43	96·63	96·83	97·02	97·22	97·42	97·61	97·81	2	4	6	8	10	12	14	16	18
9·9	98·01	98·21	98·41	98·60	98·80	99·00	99·20	99·40	99·60	99·80	2	4	6	8	10	12	14	16	18

x	0	1	2	3	4	5	6	7	8	9	1	2	3	4	5	6	7	8	9
1·0	1·0000	0050	0100	0149	0198	0247	0296	0344	0392	0440	5	10	15	20	24	29	34	39	44
1·1	1·0488	0536	0583	0630	0677	0724	0770	0817	0863	0909	5	9	14	19	23	28	33	37	42
1·2	1·0954	1000	1045	1091	1136	1180	1225	1269	1314	1358	4	9	13	18	22	27	31	36	40
1·3	1·1402	1446	1489	1533	1576	1619	1662	1705	1747	1790	4	9	13	17	22	26	30	34	39
1·4	1·1832	1874	1916	1958	2000	2042	2083	2124	2166	2207	4	8	12	17	21	25	29	33	37
1·5	1·2247	2288	2329	2369	2410	2450	2490	2530	2570	2610	4	8	12	16	20	24	28	32	36
1·6	1·2649	2689	2728	2767	2806	2845	2884	2923	2961	3000	4	8	12	16	19	23	27	31	35
1·7	1·3038	3077	3115	3153	3191	3229	3266	3304	3342	3379	4	8	11	15	19	23	26	30	34
1·8	1·3416	3454	3491	3528	3565	3601	3638	3675	3711	3748	4	7	11	15	18	22	26	29	33
1·9	1·3784	3820	3856	3892	3928	3964	4000	4036	4071	4107	4	7	11	14	18	22	25	29	32
2·0	1·4142	4177	4213	4248	4283	4318	4353	4387	4422	4457	3	7	10	14	17	21	24	28	31
2·1	1·4491	4526	4560	4595	4629	4663	4697	4731	4765	4799	3	7	10	14	17	20	24	27	31
2·2	1·4832	4866	4900	4933	4967	5000	5033	5067	5100	5133	3	7	10	13	17	20	23	27	30
2·3	1·5166	5199	5232	5264	5297	5330	5362	5395	5427	5460	3	7	10	13	16	20	23	26	29
2·4	1·5492	5524	5556	5588	5620	5652	5684	5716	5748	5780	3	6	10	13	16	19	22	26	29
2·5	1·5811	5843	5875	5906	5937	5969	6000	6031	6062	6093	3	6	9	13	16	19	22	25	28
2·6	1·6125	6155	6186	6217	6248	6279	6310	6340	6371	6401	3	6	9	12	15	18	22	25	28
2·7	1·6432	6462	6492	6523	6553	6583	6613	6643	6673	6703	3	6	9	12	15	18	21	24	27
2·8	1·6733	6763	6793	6823	6852	6882	6912	6941	6971	7000	3	6	9	12	15	18	21	24	27
2·9	1·7029	7059	7088	7117	7146	7176	7205	7234	7263	7292	3	6	9	12	15	17	20	23	26
3·0	1·7321	7349	7378	7407	7436	7464	7493	7521	7550	7578	3	6	9	11	14	17	20	23	26
3·1	1·7607	7635	7664	7692	7720	7748	7776	7804	7833	7861	3	6	8	11	14	17	20	23	25
3·2	1·7889	7916	7944	7972	8000	8028	8055	8083	8111	8138	3	6	8	11	14	17	19	22	25
3·3	1·8166	8193	8221	8248	8276	8303	8330	8358	8385	8412	3	5	8	11	14	16	19	22	25
3·4	1·8439	8466	8493	8520	8547	8574	8601	8628	8655	8682	3	5	8	11	13	16	19	22	24
3·5	1·8708	8735	8762	8788	8815	8841	8868	8894	8921	8947	3	5	8	11	13	16	19	21	24
3·6	1·8974	9000	9026	9053	9079	9105	9131	9157	9183	9209	3	5	8	10	13	16	18	21	24
3·7	1·9235	9261	9287	9313	9339	9365	9391	9416	9442	9468	3	5	8	10	13	16	18	21	23
3·8	1·9494	9519	9545	9570	9596	9621	9647	9672	9698	9723	3	5	8	10	13	15	18	20	23
3·9	1·9748	9774	9799	9824	9849	9875	9900	9925	9950	9975	3	5	8	10	13	15	18	20	23
4·0	2·0000	0025	0050	0075	0100	0125	0149	0174	0199	0224	2	5	7	10	12	15	17	20	22
4·1	2·0248	0273	0298	0322	0347	0372	0396	0421	0445	0469	2	5	7	10	12	15	17	20	22
4·2	2·0494	0518	0543	0567	0591	0616	0640	0664	0688	0712	2	5	7	10	12	15	17	19	22
4·3	2·0736	0761	0785	0809	0833	0857	0881	0905	0928	0952	2	5	7	10	12	14	17	19	22
4·4	2·0976	1000	1024	1048	1071	1095	1119	1142	1166	1190	2	5	7	9	12	14	17	19	21
4·5	2·1213	1237	1260	1284	1307	1331	1354	1378	1401	1424	2	5	7	9	12	14	16	19	21
4·6	2·1448	1471	1494	1517	1541	1564	1587	1610	1633	1656	2	5	7	9	12	14	16	19	21
4·7	2·1679	1703	1726	1749	1772	1794	1817	1840	1863	1886	2	5	7	9	11	14	16	18	21
4·8	2·1909	1932	1954	1977	2000	2023	2045	2068	2091	2113	2	5	7	9	11	14	16	18	20
4·9	2·2136	2159	2181	2204	2226	2249	2271	2293	2316	2338	2	4	7	9	11	13	16	18	20
5·0	2·2361	2383	2405	2428	2450	2472	2494	2517	2539	2561	2	4	7	9	11	13	16	18	20
5·1	2·2583	2605	2627	2650	2672	2694	2716	2738	2760	2782	2	4	7	9	11	13	15	18	20
5·2	2·2804	2825	2847	2869	2891	2913	2935	2956	2978	3000	2	4	7	9	11	13	15	17	20
5·3	2·3022	3043	3065	3087	3108	3130	3152	3173	3195	3216	2	4	6	9	11	13	15	17	19
5·4	2·3238	3259	3281	3302	3324	3345	3367	3388	3409	3431	2	4	6	9	11	13	15	17	19

SQUARE ROOTS OF NUMBERS (1 ≤ x < 10)

x	0	1	2	3	4	5	6	7	8	9	1	2	3	4	5	6	7	8	9
5·5	2·3452	3473	3495	3516	3537	3558	3580	3601	3622	3643	2	4	6	8	11	13	15	17	19
5·6	2·3664	3685	3707	3728	3749	3770	3791	3812	3833	3854	2	4	6	8	11	13	15	17	19
5·7	2·3875	3896	3917	3937	3958	3979	4000	4021	4042	4062	2	4	6	8	10	13	15	17	19
5·8	2·4083	4104	4125	4145	4166	4187	4207	4228	4249	4269	2	4	6	8	10	12	14	17	19
5·9	2·4290	4310	4331	4352	4372	4393	4413	4434	4454	4474	2	4	6	8	10	12	14	16	18
6·0	2·4495	4515	4536	4556	4576	4597	4617	4637	4658	4678	2	4	6	8	10	12	14	16	18
6·1	2·4698	4718	4739	4759	4779	4799	4819	4839	4860	4880	2	4	6	8	10	12	14	16	18
6·2	2·4900	4920	4940	4960	4980	5000	5020	5040	5060	5080	2	4	6	8	10	12	14	16	18
6·3	2·5100	5120	5140	5159	5179	5199	5219	5239	5259	5278	2	4	6	8	10	12	14	16	18
6·4	2·5298	5318	5338	5357	5377	5397	5417	5436	5456	5475	2	4	6	8	10	12	14	16	18
6·5	2·5495	5515	5534	5554	5573	5593	5612	5632	5652	5671	2	4	6	8	10	12	14	16	18
6·6	2·5690	5710	5729	5749	5768	5788	5807	5826	5846	5865	2	4	6	8	10	12	14	16	17
6·7	2·5884	5904	5923	5942	5962	5981	6000	6019	6038	6058	2	4	6	8	10	12	13	15	17
6·8	2·6077	6096	6115	6134	6153	6173	6192	6211	6230	6249	2	4	6	8	10	11	13	15	17
6·9	2·6268	6287	6306	6325	6344	6363	6382	6401	6420	6439	2	4	6	8	9	11	13	15	17
7·0	2·6458	6476	6495	6514	6533	6552	6571	6589	6608	6627	2	4	6	8	9	11	13	15	17
7·1	2·6646	6665	6683	6702	6721	6739	6758	6777	6796	6814	2	4	6	7	9	11	13	15	17
7·2	2·6833	6851	6870	6889	6907	6926	6944	6963	6981	7000	2	4	6	7	9	11	13	15	17
7·3	2·7019	7037	7055	7074	7092	7111	7129	7148	7166	7185	2	4	6	7	9	11	13	15	17
7·4	2·7203	7221	7240	7258	7276	7295	7313	7331	7350	7368	2	4	5	7	9	11	13	15	16
7·5	2·7386	7404	7423	7441	7459	7477	7495	7514	7532	7550	2	4	5	7	9	11	13	15	16
7·6	2·7568	7586	7604	7622	7641	7659	7677	7695	7713	7731	2	4	5	7	9	11	13	14	16
7·7	2·7749	7767	7785	7803	7821	7839	7857	7875	7893	7911	2	4	5	7	9	11	13	14	16
7·8	2·7928	7946	7964	7982	8000	8018	8036	8054	8071	8089	2	4	5	7	9	11	12	14	16
7·9	2·8107	8125	8142	8160	8178	8196	8213	8231	8249	8267	2	4	5	7	9	11	12	14	16
8·0	2·8284	8302	8320	8337	8355	8373	8390	8408	8425	8443	2	4	5	7	9	11	12	14	16
8·1	2·8460	8478	8496	8513	8531	8548	8566	8583	8601	8618	2	4	5	7	9	11	12	14	16
8·2	2·8636	8653	8671	8688	8705	8723	8740	8758	8775	8792	2	3	5	7	9	10	12	14	16
8·3	2·8810	8827	8844	8862	8879	8896	8914	8931	8948	8965	2	3	5	7	9	10	12	14	16
8·4	2·8983	9000	9017	9034	9052	9069	9086	9103	9120	9138	2	3	5	7	9	10	12	14	15
8·5	2·9155	9172	9189	9206	9223	9240	9257	9275	9292	9309	2	3	5	7	9	10	12	14	15
8·6	2·9326	9343	9360	9377	9394	9411	9428	9445	9462	9479	2	3	5	7	9	10	12	14	15
8·7	2·9496	9513	9530	9547	9563	9580	9597	9614	9631	9648	2	3	5	7	8	10	12	14	15
8·8	2·9665	9682	9698	9715	9732	9749	9766	9783	9799	9816	2	3	5	7	8	10	12	13	15
8·9	2·9833	9850	9866	9883	9900	9917	9933	9950	9967	9983	2	3	5	7	8	10	12	13	15
9·0	3·0000	0017	0033	0050	0067	0083	0100	0116	0133	0150	2	3	5	7	8	10	12	13	15
9·1	3·0166	0183	0199	0216	0232	0249	0265	0282	0299	0315	2	3	5	7	8	10	12	13	15
9·2	3·0332	0348	0364	0381	0397	0414	0430	0447	0463	0480	2	3	5	7	8	10	12	13	15
9·3	3·0496	0512	0529	0545	0561	0578	0594	0610	0627	0643	2	3	5	7	8	10	11	13	15
9·4	3·0659	0676	0692	0708	0725	0741	0757	0773	0790	0806	2	3	5	7	8	10	11	13	15
9·5	3·0822	0838	0854	0871	0887	0903	0919	0935	0952	0968	2	3	5	6	8	10	11	13	15
9·6	3·0984	1000	1016	1032	1048	1064	1081	1097	1113	1129	2	3	5	6	8	10	11	13	14
9·7	3·1145	1161	1177	1193	1209	1225	1241	1257	1273	1289	2	3	5	6	8	10	11	13	14
9·8	3·1305	1321	1337	1353	1369	1385	1401	1417	1432	1448	2	3	5	6	8	10	11	13	14
9·9	3·1464	1480	1496	1512	1528	1544	1559	1575	1591	1607	2	3	5	6	8	10	11	13	14

SQUARE ROOTS OF NUMBERS (10 ≤ x < 100)

x	·0	·1	·2	·3	·4	·5	·6	·7	·8	·9	1	2	3	4	5	6	7	8	9
10	3·1623	1780	1937	2094	2249	2404	2558	2711	2863	3015	15	31	46	62	77	93	108	124	139
11	3·3166	3317	3466	3615	3764	3912	4059	4205	4351	4496	15	30	44	59	74	89	103	118	133
12	3·4641	4785	4928	5071	5214	5355	5496	5637	5777	5917	14	28	43	57	71	85	99	113	128
13	3·6056	6194	6332	6469	6606	6742	6878	7014	7148	7283	14	27	41	55	68	82	95	109	123
14	3·7417	7550	7683	7815	7947	8079	8210	8341	8471	8601	13	26	39	53	66	79	92	105	118
15	3·8730	8859	8987	9115	9243	9370	9497	9623	9749	9875	13	25	38	51	64	76	89	102	114
16	4·0000	0125	0249	0373	0497	0620	0743	0866	0988	1110	12	25	37	49	62	74	86	99	111
17	4·1231	1352	1473	1593	1713	1833	1952	2071	2190	2308	12	24	36	48	60	72	84	96	108
18	4·2426	2544	2661	2778	2895	3012	3128	3243	3359	3474	12	23	35	47	58	70	81	93	105
19	4·3589	3704	3818	3932	4045	4159	4272	4385	4497	4609	11	23	34	45	57	68	79	91	102
20	4·4721	4833	4944	5056	5166	5277	5387	5497	5607	5717	11	22	33	44	55	66	77	88	100
21	4·5826	5935	6043	6152	6260	6368	6476	6583	6690	6797	11	22	32	43	54	65	76	86	97
22	4·6904	7011	7117	7223	7329	7434	7539	7645	7749	7854	11	21	32	42	53	63	74	84	95
23	4·7958	8062	8166	8270	8374	8477	8580	8683	8785	8888	10	21	31	41	52	62	72	83	93
24	4·8990	9092	9193	9295	9396	9497	9598	9699	9800	9900	10	20	30	40	51	61	71	81	91
25	5·0000	0100	0200	0299	0398	0498	0596	0695	0794	0892	10	20	30	40	50	59	69	79	89
26	5·0990	1088	1186	1284	1381	1478	1575	1672	1769	1865	10	19	29	39	49	58	68	78	88
27	5·1962	2058	2154	2249	2345	2440	2536	2631	2726	2820	10	19	29	38	48	57	67	76	86
28	5·2915	3009	3104	3198	3292	3385	3479	3572	3666	3759	9	19	28	37	47	56	66	75	84
29	5·3852	3944	4037	4129	4222	4314	4406	4498	4589	4681	9	18	28	37	46	55	64	74	83
30	5·4772	4863	4955	5045	5136	5227	5317	5408	5498	5588	9	18	27	36	45	54	63	72	82
31	5·5678	5767	5857	5946	6036	6125	6214	6303	6391	6480	9	18	27	36	45	53	62	71	80
32	5·6569	6657	6745	6833	6921	7009	7096	7184	7271	7359	9	18	26	35	44	53	61	70	79
33	5·7446	7533	7619	7706	7793	7879	7966	8052	8138	8224	9	17	26	35	43	52	61	69	78
34	5·8310	8395	8481	8566	8652	8737	8822	8907	8992	9076	9	17	26	34	43	51	60	68	77
35	5·9161	9245	9330	9414	9498	9582	9666	9749	9833	9917	8	17	25	34	42	50	59	67	76
36	6·0000	0083	0166	0249	0332	0415	0498	0581	0663	0745	8	17	25	33	41	50	58	66	75
37	6·0828	0910	0992	1074	1156	1237	1319	1400	1482	1563	8	16	25	33	41	49	57	65	74
38	6·1644	1725	1806	1887	1968	2048	2129	2209	2290	2370	8	16	24	32	40	48	56	65	73
39	6·2450	2530	2610	2690	2769	2849	2929	3008	3087	3166	8	16	24	32	40	48	56	64	72
40	6·3246	3325	3403	3482	3561	3640	3718	3797	3875	3953	8	16	24	31	39	47	55	63	71
41	6·4031	4109	4187	4265	4343	4420	4498	4576	4653	4730	8	16	23	31	39	47	54	62	70
42	6·4807	4885	4962	5038	5115	5192	5269	5345	5422	5498	8	15	23	31	38	46	54	61	69
43	6·5574	5651	5727	5803	5879	5955	6030	6106	6182	6257	8	15	23	30	38	46	53	61	68
44	6·6332	6408	6483	6558	6633	6708	6783	6858	6933	7007	7	15	22	30	37	45	52	60	67
45	6·7082	7157	7231	7305	7380	7454	7528	7602	7676	7750	7	15	22	30	37	44	52	59	67
46	6·7823	7897	7971	8044	8118	8191	8264	8337	8411	8484	7	15	22	29	37	44	51	59	66
47	6·8557	8629	8702	8775	8848	8920	8993	9065	9138	9210	7	15	22	29	36	44	51	58	65
48	6·9282	9354	9426	9498	9570	9642	9714	9785	9857	9929	7	14	22	29	36	43	50	57	65
49	7·0000	0071	0143	0214	0285	0356	0427	0498	0569	0640	7	14	21	28	36	43	50	57	64
50	7·0711	0781	0852	0922	0993	1063	1134	1204	1274	1344	7	14	21	28	35	42	49	56	63
51	7·1414	1484	1554	1624	1694	1764	1833	1903	1972	2042	7	14	21	28	35	42	49	56	63
52	7·2111	2180	2250	2319	2388	2457	2526	2595	2664	2732	7	14	21	28	35	41	48	55	62
53	7·2801	2870	2938	3007	3075	3144	3212	3280	3348	3417	7	14	21	27	34	41	48	55	62
54	7·3485	3553	3621	3689	3756	3824	3892	3959	4027	4095	7	14	20	27	34	41	47	54	61

x	·0	·1	·2	·3	·4	·5	·6	·7	·8	·9	1	2	3	4	5	6	7	8	9
55	7·4162	4229	4297	4364	4431	4498	4565	4632	4699	4766	7	13	20	27	34	40	47	54	60
56	7·4833	4900	4967	5033	5100	5166	5233	5299	5366	5432	7	13	20	27	33	40	47	53	60
57	7·5498	5565	5631	5697	5763	5829	5895	5961	6026	6092	7	13	20	26	33	40	46	53	59
58	7·6158	6223	6289	6354	6420	6485	6551	6616	6681	6746	7	13	20	26	33	39	46	52	59
59	7·6811	6877	6942	7006	7071	7136	7201	7266	7330	7395	6	13	19	26	32	39	45	52	58
60	7·7460	7524	7589	7653	7717	7782	7846	7910	7974	8038	6	13	19	26	32	39	45	51	58
61	7·8102	8166	8230	8294	8358	8422	8486	8549	8613	8677	6	13	19	26	32	38	45	51	57
62	7·8740	8804	8867	8930	8994	9057	9120	9183	9246	9310	6	13	19	25	32	38	44	51	57
63	7·9373	9436	9498	9561	9624	9687	9750	9812	9875	9937	6	13	19	25	31	38	44	50	56
64	8·0000	0062	0125	0187	0250	0312	0374	0436	0498	0561	6	12	19	25	31	37	44	50	56
65	8·0623	0685	0747	0808	0870	0932	0994	1056	1117	1179	6	12	19	25	31	37	43	49	56
66	8·1240	1302	1363	1425	1486	1548	1609	1670	1731	1792	6	12	18	25	31	37	43	49	55
67	8·1854	1915	1976	2037	2098	2158	2219	2280	2341	2401	6	12	18	24	30	37	43	49	55
68	8·2462	2523	2583	2644	2704	2765	2825	2885	2946	3006	6	12	18	24	30	36	42	48	54
69	8·3066	3126	3187	3247	3307	3367	3427	3487	3546	3606	6	12	18	24	30	36	42	48	54
70	8·3666	3726	3785	3845	3905	3964	4024	4083	4143	4202	6	12	18	24	30	36	42	48	54
71	8·4261	4321	4380	4439	4499	4558	4617	4676	4735	4794	6	12	18	24	30	35	41	47	53
72	8·4853	4912	4971	5029	5088	5147	5206	5264	5323	5381	6	12	18	23	29	35	41	47	53
73	8·5440	5499	5557	5615	5674	5732	5790	5849	5907	5965	6	12	18	23	29	35	41	47	53
74	8·6023	6081	6139	6197	6255	6313	6371	6429	6487	6545	6	12	17	23	29	35	41	46	52
75	8·6603	6660	6718	6776	6833	6891	6948	7006	7063	7121	6	12	17	23	29	35	40	46	52
76	8·7178	7235	7293	7350	7407	7464	7521	7579	7636	7693	6	11	17	23	29	34	40	46	51
77	8·7750	7807	7864	7920	7977	8034	8091	8148	8204	8261	6	11	17	23	28	34	40	45	51
78	8·8318	8374	8431	8487	8544	8600	8657	8713	8769	8826	6	11	17	23	28	34	40	45	51
79	8·8882	8938	8994	9051	9107	9163	9219	9275	9331	9387	6	11	17	22	28	34	39	45	50
80	8·9443	9499	9554	9610	9666	9722	9778	9833	9889	9944	6	11	17	22	28	33	39	45	50
81	9·0000	0056	0111	0167	0222	0277	0333	0388	0443	0499	6	11	17	22	28	33	39	44	50
82	9·0554	0609	0664	0719	0774	0830	0885	0940	0995	1049	6	11	17	22	28	33	39	44	50
83	9·1104	1159	1214	1269	1324	1378	1433	1488	1542	1597	5	11	16	22	27	33	38	44	49
84	9·1652	1706	1761	1815	1869	1924	1978	2033	2087	2141	5	11	16	22	27	33	38	44	49
85	9·2195	2250	2304	2358	2412	2466	2520	2574	2628	2682	5	11	16	22	27	32	38	43	49
86	9·2736	2790	2844	2898	2952	3005	3059	3113	3167	3220	5	11	16	22	27	32	38	43	48
87	9·3274	3327	3381	3434	3488	3541	3595	3648	3702	3755	5	11	16	21	27	32	37	43	48
88	9·3808	3862	3915	3968	4021	4074	4128	4181	4234	4287	5	11	16	21	27	32	37	43	48
89	9·4340	4393	4446	4499	4552	4604	4657	4710	4763	4816	5	11	16	21	26	32	37	42	48
90	9·4868	4921	4974	5026	5079	5131	5184	5237	5289	5341	5	11	16	21	26	32	37	42	47
91	9·5394	5446	5499	5551	5603	5656	5708	5760	5812	5864	5	10	16	21	26	31	37	42	47
92	9·5917	5969	6021	6073	6125	6177	6229	6281	6333	6385	5	10	16	21	26	31	36	42	47
93	9·6437	6488	6540	6592	6644	6695	6747	6799	6850	6902	5	10	16	21	26	31	36	41	47
94	9·6954	7005	7057	7108	7160	7211	7263	7314	7365	7417	5	10	15	21	26	31	36	41	46
95	9·7468	7519	7570	7622	7673	7724	7775	7826	7877	7929	5	10	15	20	26	31	36	41	46
96	9·7980	8031	8082	8133	8184	8234	8285	8336	8387	8438	5	10	15	20	25	31	36	41	46
97	9·8489	8539	8590	8641	8691	8742	8793	8843	8894	8944	5	10	15	20	25	30	35	41	46
98	9·8995	9045	9096	9146	9197	9247	9298	9348	9398	9448	5	10	15	20	25	30	35	40	45
99	9·9499	9549	9599	9649	9700	9750	9800	9850	9900	9950	5	10	15	20	25	30	35	40	45

CUBES

	0	1	2	3	4	5	6	7	8	9	1	2	3	4	5	6	7	8	9
1·0	1·000	1·030	1·061	1·093	1·125	1·158	1·191	1·225	1·260	1·295	3	7	10	13	16	20	23	26	30
1·1	1·331	1·368	1·405	1·443	1·482	1·521	1·561	1·602	1·643	1·685	4	8	12	16	20	24	28	31	35
1·2	1·728	1·772	1·816	1·861	1·907	1·953	2·000	2·048	2·097	2·147	5	9	14	19	23	28	33	37	42
1·3	2·197	2·248	2·300	2·353	2·406	2·460	2·515	2·571	2·628	2·686	5	11	16	22	27	33	38	43	49
1·4	2·744	2·803	2·863	2·924	2·986	3·049	3·112	3·177	3·242	3·308	6	13	19	25	31	38	44	50	56
1·5	3·375	3·443	3·512	3·582	3·652	3·724	3·796	3·870	3·944	4·020	7	14	21	29	36	43	50	57	64
1·6	4·096	4·173	4·252	4·331	4·411	4·492	4·574	4·657	4·742	4·827	8	16	24	32	41	49	57	65	73
1·7	4·913	5·000	5·088	5·178	5·268	5·359	5·452	5·545	5·640	5·735	9	18	27	37	46	55	64	73	82
1·8	5·832	5·930	6·029	6·128	6·230	6·332	6·435	6·539	6·645	6·751	10	20	31	41	51	61	71	82	92
1·9	6·859	6·968	7·078	7·189	7·301	7·415	7·530	7·645	7·762	7·881	11	23	34	45	57	68	79	91	102
2·0	8·000	8·121	8·242	8·365	8·490	8·615	8·742	8·870	8·999	9·129	13	25	38	50	63	75	88	100	113
2·1	9·261	9·394	9·528	9·664	9·800	9·938	10·078	10·218	10·360	10·503	14	28	41	55	69	83	97	110	124
2·2	10·648	10·794	10·941	11·090	11·239	11·391	11·543	11·697	11·852	12·009	15	30	45	60	76	91	106	121	136
2·3	12·167	12·326	12·487	12·649	12·813	12·978	13·144	13·312	13·481	13·652	16	33	49	66	82	99	115	132	148
2·4	13·824	13·998	14·172	14·349	14·527	14·706	14·887	15·069	15·253	15·438	18	36	54	72	90	108	126	143	161
2·5	15·625	15·813	16·003	16·194	16·387	16·581	16·777	16·975	17·174	17·374	19	39	58	78	97	117	136	155	175
2·6	17·576	17·780	17·985	18·191	18·400	18·610	18·821	19·034	19·249	19·465	21	42	63	84	105	126	147	168	189
2·7	19·683	19·903	20·124	20·346	20·571	20·797	21·025	21·254	21·485	21·718	23	45	68	90	113	136	158	181	203
2·8	21·952	22·188	22·426	22·665	22·906	23·149	23·394	23·640	23·888	24·138	24	49	73	97	121	146	170	194	219
2·9	24·389	24·642	24·897	25·154	25·412	25·672	25·934	26·198	26·464	26·731	26	52	78	104	130	156	182	208	234
3·0	27·000	27·271	27·544	27·818	28·094	28·373	28·653	28·934	29·218	29·504	28	56	83	111	139	167	195	223	250
3·1	29·791	30·080	30·371	30·664	30·959	31·256	31·554	31·855	32·157	32·462	30	59	89	119	148	178	208	237	267
3·2	32·768	33·076	33·386	33·698	34·012	34·328	34·646	34·966	35·288	35·611	32	63	95	126	158	190	221	253	284
3·3	35·937	36·265	36·594	36·926	37·260	37·595	37·933	38·273	38·614	38·958	34	67	101	134	168	201	235	269	302
3·4	39·304	39·652	40·002	40·354	40·708	41·064	41·422	41·782	42·144	42·509	36	71	107	142	178	214	249	285	320
3·5	42·87	43·24	43·61	43·99	44·36	44·74	45·12	45·50	45·88	46·27	4	8	11	15	19	23	26	30	34
3·6	46·66	47·05	47·44	47·83	48·23	48·63	49·03	49·43	49·84	50·24	4	8	12	16	20	24	28	32	36
3·7	50·65	51·06	51·48	51·90	52·31	52·73	53·16	53·58	54·01	54·44	4	8	13	17	21	25	29	34	38
3·8	54·87	55·31	55·74	56·18	56·62	57·07	57·51	57·96	58·41	58·86	4	9	13	18	22	27	31	35	40
3·9	59·32	59·78	60·24	60·70	61·16	61·63	62·10	62·57	63·04	63·52	5	9	14	19	23	28	33	37	42
4·0	64·00	64·48	64·96	65·45	65·94	66·43	66·92	67·42	67·92	68·42	5	10	15	20	25	29	34	39	44
4·1	68·92	69·43	69·93	70·44	70·96	71·47	71·99	72·51	73·03	73·56	5	10	15	21	26	31	36	41	46
4·2	74·09	74·62	75·15	75·69	76·23	76·77	77·31	77·85	78·40	78·95	5	11	16	22	27	32	38	43	49
4·3	79·51	80·06	80·62	81·18	81·75	82·31	82·88	83·45	84·03	84·60	6	11	17	23	28	34	40	45	51
4·4	85·18	85·77	86·35	86·94	87·53	88·12	88·72	89·31	89·92	90·52	6	12	18	24	30	36	41	47	53
4·5	91·12	91·73	92·35	92·96	93·58	94·20	94·82	95·44	96·07	96·70	6	12	19	25	31	37	43	50	56
4·6	97·34	97·97	98·61	99·25	99·90	100·54	101·19	101·85	102·50	103·16	6	13	19	26	32	39	45	52	58
4·7	103·82	104·49	105·15	105·82	106·50	107·17	107·85	108·53	109·22	109·90	7	14	20	27	34	41	47	54	61
4·8	110·59	111·28	111·98	112·68	113·38	114·08	114·79	115·50	116·21	116·93	7	14	21	28	35	42	49	56	63
4·9	117·65	118·37	119·10	119·82	120·55	121·29	122·02	122·76	123·51	124·25	7	15	22	29	37	44	51	59	66
5·0	125·00	125·75	126·51	127·26	128·02	128·79	129·55	130·32	131·10	131·87	8	15	23	31	38	46	53	61	69
5·1	132·65	133·43	134·22	135·01	135·80	136·59	137·39	138·19	138·99	139·80	8	16	24	32	40	48	56	64	71
5·2	140·61	141·42	142·24	143·06	143·88	144·70	145·53	146·36	147·20	148·04	8	17	25	33	41	50	58	66	74
5·3	148·88	149·72	150·57	151·42	152·27	153·13	153·99	154·85	155·72	156·59	9	17	26	34	43	51	60	69	77
5·4	157·46	158·34	159·22	160·10	160·99	161·88	162·77	163·67	164·57	165·47	9	18	27	36	44	53	62	71	80

CUBES

	0	1	2	3	4	5	6	7	8	9	1	2	3	4	5	6	7	8	9
5·5	166·4	167·3	168·2	169·1	170·0	171·0	171·9	172·8	173·7	174·7	1	2	3	4	5	6	6	7	8
5·6	175·6	176·6	177·5	178·5	179·4	180·4	181·3	182·3	183·3	184·2	1	2	3	4	5	6	7	8	9
5·7	185·2	186·2	187·1	188·1	189·1	190·1	191·1	192·1	193·1	194·1	1	2	3	4	5	6	7	8	9
5·8	195·1	196·1	197·1	198·2	199·2	200·2	201·2	202·3	203·3	204·3	1	2	3	4	5	6	7	8	9
5·9	205·4	206·4	207·5	208·5	209·6	210·6	211·7	212·8	213·8	214·9	1	2	3	4	5	6	7	8	10
6·0	216·0	217·1	218·2	219·3	220·3	221·4	222·5	223·6	224·8	225·9	1	2	3	4	5	7	8	9	10
6·1	227·0	228·1	229·2	230·3	231·5	232·6	233·7	234·9	236·0	237·2	1	2	3	5	6	7	8	9	10
6·2	238·3	239·5	240·6	241·8	243·0	244·1	245·3	246·5	247·7	248·9	1	2	4	5	6	7	8	9	11
6·3	250·0	251·2	252·4	253·6	254·8	256·0	257·3	258·5	259·7	260·9	1	2	4	5	6	7	8	10	11
6·4	262·1	263·4	264·6	265·8	267·1	268·3	269·6	270·8	272·1	273·4	1	2	4	5	6	7	9	10	11
6·5	274·6	275·9	277·2	278·4	279·7	281·0	282·3	283·6	284·9	286·2	1	3	4	5	6	8	9	10	12
6·6	287·5	288·8	290·1	291·4	292·8	294·1	295·4	296·7	298·1	299·4	1	3	4	5	7	8	9	11	12
6·7	300·8	302·1	303·5	304·8	306·2	307·5	308·9	310·3	311·7	313·0	1	3	4	5	7	8	10	11	12
6·8	314·4	315·8	317·2	318·6	320·0	321·4	322·8	324·2	325·7	327·1	1	3	4	6	7	8	10	11	13
6·9	328·5	329·9	331·4	332·8	334·3	335·7	337·2	338·6	340·1	341·5	1	3	4	6	7	9	10	12	13
7·0	343·0	344·5	345·9	347·4	348·9	350·4	351·9	353·4	354·9	356·4	1	3	4	6	7	9	10	12	13
7·1	357·9	359·4	360·9	362·5	364·0	365·5	367·1	368·6	370·1	371·7	2	3	5	6	8	9	11	12	14
7·2	373·2	374·8	376·4	377·9	379·5	381·1	382·7	384·2	385·8	387·4	2	3	5	6	8	9	11	13	14
7·3	389·0	390·6	392·2	393·8	395·4	397·1	398·7	400·3	401·9	403·6	2	3	5	6	8	10	11	13	15
7·4	405·2	406·9	408·5	410·2	411·8	413·5	415·2	416·8	418·5	420·2	2	3	5	7	8	10	12	13	15
7·5	421·9	423·6	425·3	427·0	428·7	430·4	432·1	433·8	435·5	437·2	2	3	5	7	9	10	12	14	15
7·6	439·0	440·7	442·5	444·2	445·9	447·7	449·5	451·2	453·0	454·8	2	4	5	7	9	11	12	14	16
7·7	456·5	458·3	460·1	461·9	463·7	465·5	467·3	469·1	470·9	472·7	2	4	5	7	9	11	13	14	16
7·8	474·6	476·4	478·2	480·0	481·9	483·7	485·6	487·4	489·3	491·2	2	4	6	7	9	11	13	15	17
7·9	493·0	494·9	496·8	498·7	500·6	502·5	504·4	506·3	508·2	510·1	2	4	6	8	9	11	13	15	17
8·0	512·0	513·9	515·8	517·8	519·7	521·7	523·6	525·6	527·5	529·5	2	4	6	8	10	12	14	16	17
8·1	531·4	533·4	535·4	537·4	539·4	541·3	543·3	545·3	547·3	549·4	2	4	6	8	10	12	14	16	18
8·2	551·4	553·4	555·4	557·4	559·5	561·5	563·6	565·6	567·7	569·7	2	4	6	8	10	12	14	16	18
8·3	571·8	573·9	575·9	578·0	580·1	582·2	584·3	586·4	588·5	590·6	2	4	6	8	10	13	15	17	19
8·4	592·7	594·8	596·9	599·1	601·2	603·4	605·5	607·6	609·8	612·0	2	4	6	9	11	13	15	17	19
8·5	614·1	616·3	618·5	620·7	622·8	625·0	627·2	629·4	631·6	633·8	2	4	7	9	11	13	15	18	20
8·6	636·1	638·3	640·5	642·7	645·0	647·2	649·5	651·7	654·0	656·2	2	4	7	9	11	13	16	18	20
8·7	658·5	660·8	663·1	665·3	667·6	669·9	672·2	674·5	676·8	679·2	2	5	7	9	11	14	16	18	21
8·8	681·5	683·8	686·1	688·5	690·8	693·2	695·5	697·9	700·2	702·6	2	5	7	9	12	14	16	19	21
8·9	705·0	707·3	709·7	712·1	714·5	716·9	719·3	721·7	724·2	726·6	2	5	7	10	12	14	17	19	22
9·0	729·0	731·4	733·9	736·3	738·8	741·2	743·7	746·1	748·6	751·1	2	5	7	10	12	15	17	20	22
9·1	753·6	756·1	758·6	761·0	763·6	766·1	768·6	771·1	773·6	776·2	3	5	8	10	13	15	18	20	23
9·2	778·7	781·2	783·8	786·3	788·9	791·5	794·0	796·6	799·2	801·8	3	5	8	10	13	15	18	21	23
9·3	804·4	807·0	809·6	812·2	814·8	817·4	820·0	822·7	825·3	827·9	3	5	8	10	13	16	18	21	24
9·4	830·6	833·2	835·9	838·6	841·2	843·9	846·6	849·3	852·0	854·7	3	5	8	11	13	16	19	21	24
9·5	857·4	860·1	862·8	865·5	868·3	871·0	873·7	876·5	879·2	882·0	3	5	8	11	14	16	19	22	25
9·6	884·7	887·5	890·3	893·1	895·8	898·6	901·4	904·2	907·0	909·9	3	6	8	11	14	17	20	22	25
9·7	912·7	915·5	918·3	921·2	924·0	926·9	929·7	932·6	935·4	938·3	3	6	9	11	14	17	20	23	26
9·8	941·2	944·1	947·0	949·9	952·8	955·7	958·6	961·5	964·4	967·4	3	6	9	12	15	17	20	23	26
9·9	970·3	973·2	976·2	979·1	982·1	985·1	988·0	991·0	994·0	997·0	3	6	9	12	15	18	21	24	27

RECIPROCALS

	0	1	2	3	4	5	6	7	8	9	1	2	3	4	5	6	7	8	9
1·0	1·0000	9901	9804	9709	9615	9524	9434	9346	9259	9174	9	18	28	37	46	55	64	73	83
1·1	0·9091	9009	8929	8850	8772	8696	8621	8547	8475	8403	8	15	23	31	38	46	53	61	69
1·2	0·8333	8264	8197	8130	8065	8000	7937	7874	7813	7752	6	13	19	26	32	39	45	52	58
1·3	0·7692	7634	7576	7519	7463	7407	7353	7299	7246	7194	6	11	17	22	28	33	39	44	50
1·4	0·7143	7092	7042	6993	6944	6897	6849	6803	6757	6711	5	10	14	19	24	29	34	38	43
1·5	0·6667	6623	6579	6536	6494	6452	6410	6369	6329	6289	4	8	13	17	21	25	29	34	38
1·6	0·6250	6211	6173	6135	6098	6061	6024	5988	5952	5917	4	7	11	15	18	22	26	30	33
1·7	0·5882	5848	5814	5780	5747	5714	5682	5650	5618	5587	3	7	10	13	16	20	23	26	30
1·8	0·5556	5525	5495	5464	5435	5405	5376	5348	5319	5291	3	6	9	12	15	18	21	24	26
1·9	0·5263	5236	5208	5181	5155	5128	5102	5076	5051	5025	3	5	8	11	13	16	19	21	24
2·0	0·5000	4975	4950	4926	4902	4878	4854	4831	4808	4785	2	5	7	10	12	14	17	19	22
2·1	0·4762	4739	4717	4695	4673	4651	4630	4608	4587	4566	2	4	7	9	11	13	15	17	20
2·2	0·4545	4525	4505	4484	4464	4444	4425	4405	4386	4367	2	4	6	8	10	12	14	16	18
2·3	0·4348	4329	4310	4292	4274	4255	4237	4219	4202	4184	2	4	5	7	9	11	13	15	16
2·4	0·4167	4149	4132	4115	4098	4082	4065	4049	4032	4016	2	3	5	7	8	10	12	13	15
2·5	0·4000	3984	3968	3953	3937	3922	3906	3891	3876	3861	2	3	5	6	8	9	11	12	14
2·6	0·3846	3831	3817	3802	3788	3774	3759	3745	3731	3717	1	3	4	6	7	9	10	11	13
2·7	0·3704	3690	3676	3663	3650	3636	3623	3610	3597	3584	1	3	4	5	7	8	9	11	12
2·8	0·3571	3559	3546	3534	3521	3509	3497	3484	3472	3460	1	2	4	5	6	7	9	10	11
2·9	0·3448	3436	3425	3413	3401	3390	3378	3367	3356	3344	1	2	3	5	6	7	8	9	10
3·0	0·3333	3322	3311	3300	3289	3279	3268	3257	3247	3236	1	2	3	4	5	6	8	9	10
3·1	0·3226	3215	3205	3195	3185	3175	3165	3155	3145	3135	1	2	3	4	5	6	7	8	9
3·2	0·3125	3115	3106	3096	3086	3077	3067	3058	3049	3040	1	2	3	4	5	6	7	8	9
3·3	0·3030	3021	3012	3003	2994	2985	2976	2967	2959	2950	1	2	3	4	4	5	6	7	8
3·4	0·2941	2933	2924	2915	2907	2899	2890	2882	2874	2865	1	2	3	3	4	5	6	7	8
3·5	0·2857	2849	2841	2833	2825	2817	2809	2801	2793	2786	1	2	2	3	4	5	6	6	7
3·6	0·2778	2770	2762	2755	2747	2740	2732	2725	2717	2710	1	2	2	3	4	5	5	6	7
3·7	0·2703	2695	2688	2681	2674	2667	2660	2653	2646	2639	1	1	2	3	4	4	5	6	6
3·8	0·2632	2625	2618	2611	2604	2597	2591	2584	2577	2571	1	1	2	3	3	4	5	5	6
3·9	0·2564	2558	2551	2545	2538	2532	2525	2519	2513	2506	1	1	2	3	3	4	4	5	6
4·0	0·2500	2494	2488	2481	2475	2469	2463	2457	2451	2445	1	1	2	2	3	4	4	5	6
4·1	0·2439	2433	2427	2421	2415	2410	2404	2398	2392	2387	1	1	2	2	3	3	4	5	5
4·2	0·2381	2375	2370	2364	2358	2353	2347	2342	2336	2331	1	1	2	2	3	3	4	4	5
4·3	0·2326	2320	2315	2309	2304	2299	2294	2288	2283	2278	1	1	2	2	3	3	4	4	5
4·4	0·2273	2268	2262	2257	2252	2247	2242	2237	2232	2227	1	1	2	2	3	3	4	4	5
4·5	0·2222	2217	2212	2208	2203	2198	2193	2188	2183	2179	0	1	1	2	2	3	3	4	4
4·6	0·2174	2169	2165	2160	2155	2151	2146	2141	2137	2132	0	1	1	2	2	3	3	4	4
4·7	0·2128	2123	2119	2114	2110	2105	2101	2096	2092	2088	0	1	1	2	2	3	3	4	4
4·8	0·2083	2079	2075	2070	2066	2062	2058	2053	2049	2045	0	1	1	2	2	3	3	3	4
4·9	0·2041	2037	2033	2028	2024	2020	2016	2012	2008	2004	0	1	1	2	2	2	3	3	4
5·0	0·2000	1996	1992	1988	1984	1980	1976	1972	1969	1965	0	1	1	2	2	3	3	3	4
5·1	0·1961	1957	1953	1949	1946	1942	1938	1934	1931	1927	0	1	1	2	2	2	3	3	3
5·2	0·1923	1919	1916	1912	1908	1905	1901	1898	1894	1890	0	1	1	1	2	2	3	3	3
5·3	0·1887	1883	1880	1876	1873	1869	1866	1862	1859	1855	0	1	1	1	2	2	3	3	3
5·4	0·1852	1848	1845	1842	1838	1835	1832	1828	1825	1821	0	1	1	1	2	2	2	3	3
	0	1	2	3	4	5	6	7	8	9	1	2	3	4	5	6	7	8	9

RECIPROCALS

	0	1	2	3	4	5	6	7	8	9	1	2	3	4	5	6	7	8	9
5·5	0·1818	1815	1812	1808	1805	1802	1799	1795	1792	1789	0	1	1	1	2	2	2	3	3
5·6	0·1786	1783	1779	1776	1773	1770	1767	1764	1761	1757	0	1	1	1	2	2	2	3	3
5·7	0·1754	1751	1748	1745	1742	1739	1736	1733	1730	1727	0	1	1	1	2	2	2	2	3
5·8	0·1724	1721	1718	1715	1712	1709	1706	1704	1701	1698	0	1	1	1	1	2	2	2	3
5·9	0·1695	1692	1689	1686	1684	1681	1678	1675	1672	1669	0	1	1	1	1	2	2	2	3
6·0	0·1667	1664	1661	1658	1656	1653	1650	1647	1645	1642	0	1	1	1	1	2	2	2	2
6·1	0·1639	1637	1634	1631	1629	1626	1623	1621	1618	1616	0	1	1	1	1	2	2	2	2
6·2	0·1613	1610	1608	1605	1603	1600	1597	1595	1592	1590	0	1	1	1	1	2	2	2	2
6·3	0·1587	1585	1582	1580	1577	1575	1572	1570	1567	1565	0	0	1	1	1	1	2	2	2
6·4	0·1563	1560	1558	1555	1553	1550	1548	1546	1543	1541	0	0	1	1	1	1	2	2	2
6·5	0·1538	1536	1534	1531	1529	1527	1524	1522	1520	1517	0	0	1	1	1	1	2	2	2
6·6	0·1515	1513	1511	1508	1506	1504	1502	1499	1497	1495	0	0	1	1	1	1	2	2	2
6·7	0·1493	1490	1488	1486	1484	1481	1479	1477	1475	1473	0	0	1	1	1	1	2	2	2
6·8	0·1471	1468	1466	1464	1462	1460	1458	1456	1453	1451	0	0	1	1	1	1	1	2	2
6·9	0·1449	1447	1445	1443	1441	1439	1437	1435	1433	1431	0	0	1	1	1	1	1	2	2
7·0	0·1429	1427	1425	1422	1420	1418	1416	1414	1412	1410	0	0	1	1	1	1	1	2	2
7·1	0·1408	1406	1404	1403	1401	1399	1397	1395	1393	1391	0	0	1	1	1	1	1	2	2
7·2	0·1389	1387	1385	1383	1381	1379	1377	1376	1374	1372	0	0	1	1	1	1	1	2	2
7·3	0·1370	1368	1366	1364	1362	1361	1359	1357	1355	1353	0	0	1	1	1	1	1	1	2
7·4	0·1351	1350	1348	1346	1344	1342	1340	1339	1337	1335	0	0	1	1	1	1	1	1	2
7·5	0·1333	1332	1330	1328	1326	1325	1323	1321	1319	1318	0	0	1	1	1	1	1	1	2
7·6	0·1316	1314	1312	1311	1309	1307	1305	1304	1302	1300	0	0	1	1	1	1	1	1	2
7·7	0·1299	1297	1295	1294	1292	1290	1289	1287	1285	1284	0	0	1	1	1	1	1	1	2
7·8	0·1282	1280	1279	1277	1276	1274	1272	1271	1269	1267	0	0	0	1	1	1	1	1	1
7·9	0·1266	1264	1263	1261	1259	1258	1256	1255	1253	1252	0	0	0	1	1	1	1	1	1
8·0	0·1250	1248	1247	1245	1244	1242	1241	1239	1238	1236	0	0	0	1	1	1	1	1	1
8·1	0·1235	1233	1232	1230	1229	1227	1225	1224	1222	1221	0	0	0	1	1	1	1	1	1
8·2	0·1220	1218	1217	1215	1214	1212	1211	1209	1208	1206	0	0	0	1	1	1	1	1	1
8·3	0·1205	1203	1202	1200	1199	1198	1196	1195	1193	1192	0	0	0	1	1	1	1	1	1
8·4	0·1190	1189	1188	1186	1185	1183	1182	1181	1179	1178	0	0	0	1	1	1	1	1	1
8·5	0·1176	1175	1174	1172	1171	1170	1168	1167	1166	1164	0	0	0	1	1	1	1	1	1
8·6	0·1163	1161	1160	1159	1157	1156	1155	1153	1152	1151	0	0	0	1	1	1	1	1	1
8·7	0·1149	1148	1147	1145	1144	1143	1142	1140	1139	1138	0	0	0	1	1	1	1	1	1
8·8	0·1136	1135	1134	1133	1131	1130	1129	1127	1126	1125	0	0	0	1	1	1	1	1	1
8·9	0·1124	1122	1121	1120	1119	1117	1116	1115	1114	1112	0	0	0	0	1	1	1	1	1
9·0	0·1111	1110	1109	1107	1106	1105	1104	1103	1101	1100	0	0	0	0	1	1	1	1	1
9·1	0·1099	1098	1096	1095	1094	1093	1092	1091	1089	1088	0	0	0	0	1	1	1	1	1
9·2	0·1087	1086	1085	1083	1082	1081	1080	1079	1078	1076	0	0	0	0	1	1	1	1	1
9·3	0·1075	1074	1073	1072	1071	1070	1068	1067	1066	1065	0	0	0	0	1	1	1	1	1
9·4	0·1064	1063	1062	1060	1059	1058	1057	1056	1055	1054	0	0	0	0	1	1	1	1	1
9·5	0·1053	1052	1050	1049	1048	1047	1046	1045	1044	1043	0	0	0	0	1	1	1	1	1
9·6	0·1042	1041	1040	1038	1037	1036	1035	1034	1033	1032	0	0	0	0	1	1	1	1	1
9·7	0·1031	1030	1029	1028	1027	1026	1025	1024	1022	1021	0	0	0	0	1	1	1	1	1
9·8	0·1020	1019	1018	1017	1016	1015	1014	1013	1012	1011	0	0	0	0	1	1	1	1	1
9·9	0·1010	1009	1008	1007	1006	1005	1004	1003	1002	1001	0	0	0	0	1	1	1	1	1
	0	1	2	3	4	5	6	7	8	9	1	2	3	4	5	6	7	8	9

LOGARITHMS OF FACTORIALS

x	$\log_{10}x!$	x	$\log_{10}x!$	x	$\log_{10}x!$	x	$\log_{10}x!$
1	0·0000	26	26·6056	51	66·1906	76	111·2754
2	0·3010	27	28·0370	52	67·9066	77	113·1619
3	0·7782	28	29·4841	53	69·6309	78	115·0540
4	1·3802	29	30·9465	54	71·3633	79	116·9516
5	2·0792	30	32·4237	55	73·1037	80	118·8547
6	2·8573	31	33·9150	56	74·8519	81	120·7632
7	3·7024	32	35·4202	57	76·6077	82	122·6770
8	4·6055	33	36·9387	58	78·3712	83	124·5961
9	5·5598	34	38·4702	59	80·1420	84	126·5204
10	6·5598	35	40·0142	60	81·9202	85	128·4498
11	7·6012	36	41·5705	61	83·7055	86	130·3843
12	8·6803	37	43·1387	62	85·4979	87	132·3238
13	9·7943	38	44·7185	63	87·2972	88	134·2683
14	10·9404	39	46·3096	64	89·1034	89	136·2177
15	12·1165	40	47·9116	65	90·9163	90	138·1719
16	13·3206	41	49·5244	66	92·7359	91	140·1310
17	14·5511	42	51·1477	67	94·5619	92	142·0948
18	15·8063	43	52·7811	68	96·3945	93	144·0632
19	17·0851	44	54·4246	69	98·2333	94	146·0364
20	18·3861	45	56·0778	70	100·0784	95	148·0141
21	19·7083	46	57·7406	71	101·9297	96	149·9964
22	21·0508	47	59·4127	72	103·7870	97	151·9831
23	22·4125	48	61·0939	73	105·6503	98	153·9744
24	23·7927	49	62·7841	74	107·5196	99	155·9700
25	25·1906	50	64·4831	75	109·3946	100	157·9700

If x is greater than 100, factorials may be obtained from the series:

$$\log_{10}x! = 0·61624 + (x+\tfrac{1}{2})(\log_{10}x - 0·4342945) + 0·0362/x - \ldots.$$

BINOMIAL COEFFICIENTS $\binom{n}{i}$

n \ i	0	1	2	3	4	5	6	7	8	9	10
1	1	1									
2	1	2	1								
3	1	3	3	1							
4	1	4	6	4	1						
5	1	5	10	10	5	1					
6	1	6	15	20	15	6	1				
7	1	7	21	35	35	21	7	1			
8	1	8	28	56	70	56	28	8	1		
9	1	9	36	84	126	126	84	36	9	1	
10	1	10	45	120	210	252	210	120	45	10	1
11	1	11	55	165	330	462	462	330	165	55	11
12	1	12	66	220	495	792	924	792	495	220	66
13	1	13	78	286	715	1287	1716	1716	1287	715	286
14	1	14	91	364	1001	2002	3003	3432	3003	2002	1001
15	1	15	105	455	1365	3003	5005	6435	6435	5005	3003
16	1	16	120	560	1820	4368	8008	11440	12870	11440	8008
17	1	17	136	680	2380	6188	12376	19448	24310	24310	19448
18	1	18	153	816	3060	8568	18564	31824	43758	48620	43758
19	1	19	171	969	3876	11628	27132	50388	75582	92378	92378
20	1	20	190	1140	4845	15504	38760	77520	125970	167960	184756